ETHICS OF DECISION

AN INTRODUCTION TO CHRISTIAN ETHICS

ETHICS
OF
DECISION

By
George W. Forell

FORTRESS PRESS   PHILADELPHIA

Second printing 1960
First paperback edition 1961
Second printing 1962
Third printing 1965
Fourth printing 1966
Fifth printing 1967
Sixth printing 1970
Seventh printing 1975
Eighth printing 1980

Library of Congress Catalog Card Number 55-7767
ISBN 0-8006-1770-3

8422C80   Printed in the United States of America   1-1770

PREFACE

This little book is planned to furnish a short introduction to Christian ethics. Its objective is to help the reader to come to a clearer understanding of the meaning of the Christian life in our age. For this reason the Christian life is presented against the background and within the context of various other contemporary efforts to understand the meaning of human existence.

An effort has been made, especially in the first part, to look at the possible alternatives to the Christian life. It is the basic assumption of this approach that every man, and especially every educated person, must find some guiding principle that will enable him to live a coherent life. This principle of integration may be found in any number of contemporary ideologies. In any case it will determine the ethics of the person who chooses it. The Christian faith makes one way of life possible. It presents an alternative to the other ideologies of our age. In the modern world, however, this Christian alternative is frequently not presented at all. In any case it is not offered as a serious alternative to "pragmatism," "naturalism," "relativism," or "positivism," but at best as some sentimental glue of society for those who cannot follow the logical arguments of the advocates of the other alternatives. Yet since Christianity has been to many people of all levels of intelligence through many centuries the only true way of life, it deserves a fair hearing. It is hoped that the following pages will help a little to clarify the way of life which is rooted in the faith that "God was in Christ reconciling the world unto himself."

The author would like to express his gratitude to the many friends who read the manuscript and made helpful suggestions.

Above all, the author is indebted to his wife, Betty, to whom this book is dedicated.

Acknowledgment is made to the following publishers for their kind permission to quote from copyrighted sources: The Macmillan Company, New York: Rudolf Otto, *Mysticism East and West* and C. S. Lewis, *Christian Behaviour*; The Philosophical Library, New York: Simone de Beauvoir, *The Ethics of Ambiguity*; Princeton University Press, Princeton: Robert Bretall, *A Kierkegaard Anthology*; Random House, New York: *The Philosophy of Nietzsche* and *Selected Papers of Bertrand Russell*; The Ronald Press Company, New York: Charles H. Patterson, *Moral Standards*.

Iowa City Iowa
Ascension Day 1955   G. W. F.

CONTENTS

PART II
The Life of Man Under the Gospel

INTRODUCTION

The crucial question confronting our age is the question of ethics. How are we to establish right and wrong? How can we tell good from evil? No doubt this problem has always been important. However, in other ages the answer seemed far simpler. People assumed that they had the answer. They were sure that the moral laws of their society were valid. There might be perverse individuals who habitually transgressed against these laws, but everybody was convinced that this was the fault of these people and not the fault of the laws.

Even if all people had to admit that they occasionally failed to live up to the moral standards of their society, they considered this a reflection on their own imperfection and not on the validity of the moral law. When Socrates talked with Euthyphro about the nature of piety more than two thousand years ago, he asserted confidently that nobody would argue that an evil-doer should not be punished. People denied then as now that they were evil-doers, that they had committed any crimes, but they never claimed that the guilty should not be punished, that there is in fact no right or wrong.

Similarly, the standards of right and wrong of the Kwakiutl Indians of Vancouver Island on the northwest coast of America may have differed profoundly from our ethical standards. But the Kwakiutl Indians never questioned the validity of their ethical norms. Though man was always questioned by his ethical laws, these ethical laws were rarely questioned by man.

It has been left to our age to deny the possibility of guilt. We are not sure that there is such a thing as right and wrong or good and bad. And this complete uncertainty about moral values is at the root of the terrible confusion of our age. This ethical chaos is the ultimate cause of all our other divisions and conflicts. Because of our uncertainty about the standards of right and wrong, a world which in some ways is more united than it has ever been is simultaneously also divided as never before.

In many ways the world in which we live is one. This is true technically, economically and geographically. Science uses a universal language of mathematical symbols and measurements. The discoveries of a scientist today are tomorrow the universal property of all scientists. This unity seems to be a fact of life that politicians and soldiers cannot change. The atom bomb was a scientific development in which people of a dozen nationalities had a share. It could not be kept a "national secret." Scientifically and technically, the world is one.

This is equally true in the realm of economics. We

are dependent upon the economic resources of almost every other country in the world. To make the clothes we wear, the cars we drive, the homes we live in, materials from all over the world are used. Economic disturbances in Brazil affect the price of your cup of coffee. And on developments in the Near East may depend whether or not you can drive your car.

Geographic distances have dwindled into utter insignificance. I had a student who flew a plane all over the world on weekends and was in class on Tuesday as if he had never been away. It takes less effort and time to go to Europe or Asia today than it used to take to visit relatives in a near-by town one hundred years ago. Ever faster means of transportation make this world geographically one: a world that was once divided by rivers, mountains, and oceans.

Yet in spite of this material oneness, our world is more divided spiritually than ever before. It may have been difficult for people to travel from Russia to Britain in the seventeenth century, but when they arrived after their long trip they came to people who believed in the same basic values, who believed that there is one God and that the Ten Commandments are the basic expression of his law for mankind. Today you have only to cross the hall in your apartment house, and the people on the other side may live in an utterly different world; a world in which there is no God, no divine law, where only self-interest, animal instincts, and the "survival of the fittest" rule. Many people today believe that right is merely what is useful to their group, and that the moral law is the codified self-interest of the people in power. There are as many worlds as there are such groups who believe that they are a law unto themselves.

Though materially one world, the anarchy of values has divided this world into an ever-increasing number of worlds which do not understand one another at all. We may use the same scientific language, depend economically upon each other, and be able to travel speedily from one place to the next, yet we live more and more in different worlds.

When I was a boy, I learned that Germans had invented the telephone and the airplane. In America, I learned that Americans had invented them. I understand that in Russia they learn that the inventors were Russians. It may not really matter who actually invented these devices, but this confusion about something which should be fairly easy to establish shows how our world is dividing into different worlds where even the "facts" are no longer the same. To be a Communist is a crime in the United States; it is a virtue in Russia. To believe in capitalism is a crime in Russia and a virtue in America. Social democracy is frowned on in Russia and America, but it is just the thing in Sweden.

This is indeed one world only materially. Spiritually it is more divided than ever in history. The cause of our confusion is the chaos of values and moral standards. This is clearly shown in the realm of faith. There is no overwhelming, all-embracing faith that dominates our civilization. There was a time in Europe and also in certain parts of America when you could safely say that Christianity dominated the life of all people. Of course that did not mean that in those days all people were Christians. But in the Europe of the twelfth century there was no part of life that was not in some way related to Christian values. You could say the same about Geneva of the sixteenth century, Scotland in the time of John Knox, or the colonies of the "pilgrim fathers."

Not only Christianity supplied such culture-dominating value structures at various periods of history. Mohammedanism, Hinduism, Buddhism did the same. There have been many times when the world—all the territory that people knew to exist, the known world at that time—was dominated by one faith.

Our world is not in fact dominated by such a faith. Hinduism does not dominate India. When you speak to a modern Indian, he appears as secularized as his American counterpart. The Christian value structure does not dominate Europe or America. This is merely a convenient illusion. There is no one overwhelming, all-embracing faith that would give meaning to the life of men everywhere.

But again we are involved in a peculiar self-contradiction. While this one faith is lacking, we have more faiths than people had at any other time—no real faith and innumerable "ersatz" faiths. This is easy to see in other people. The Germans who believed in blood and soil—German blood and soil to be sure—were a good example. They substituted faith in their race and in one man, Hitler, who for all practical purposes was deified, for their former Christian faith.

The same can be said about Russia. Communism is a religion which has everything any religion ever had except a real god. It is a substitute religion. Among our contemporaries many have become Communists because man needs a religion and their education had destroyed their faith in all traditional religions. Men like Chambers, Hiss, or Klaus Fuchs did not become Communists for money or prestige. These and many others became Communists because man is a believing being. If there is no Christian faith in his heart, something else will take its place. In the case of Chambers, Hiss and Fuchs, it was communism.

A number of these religious converts to communism who became disillusioned with the Communist religion have written a book which expresses this disillusionment, *The God That Failed*. Some of the authors are Richard Wright, Arthur Koestler, and Ignazio Silone. They all reveal that the world which has no overwhelming faith will be dominated by "ersatz" religions, the substitute faiths that take the place of true faith.

It is typical of our confusion of values that faith in God has been replaced by faith in various devices, ideas, and personalities of men. People who no longer believe in the Saviour make up their own saviours, and worship and glorify them with idolatrous zeal. These substitute faiths may appear in different versions in different parts of the world, but everywhere we see the

same chaos of values. Trust in man and his achieve-
ments has replaced a unifying and integrating faith
in God.

Sometimes an outsider can see this better than we
can ourselves. Professor Arnold Nash told once about
an African chieftain's son, a very brilliant young fellow,
who came to study in England. After he had been
there for a while he told Nash that the English are
polytheists. It turned out that he meant it literally.
Modern man has many gods, many faiths that all exist
together, no overpowering faith that controls everything. This young African scholar said that he had
met people who were fine church members, but they
said, "Business is business." The god of business
existed with his standards next to the God of their
church. They worshiped at both shrines, only much
more often at the shrine of the god of business. Or
there are the people who say, "Politics is politics."
Otherwise they are church members, but politics has
its own values and rules and they are not found in the
New Testament. And you mustn't mix politics and
Christianity. There are others who claim, "Education
is education." It is an endeavor completely apart from
all others. And certainly Christianity should not be
brought in to confuse the work of the educators!

This young African had met a lady who carved little
wooden pieces. He asked why she did it. Did she
want to sell them? No! Did she want to exhibit them?
No! She said, "You know, art for art's sake. Don't you
understand?" And the African, who did not understand,

realized that the white man had just as many gods whom he worshiped simultaneously as the polytheistic tribes of Africa—business, politics, education, art, and many others.

It is true that we do not have the faith that would make our life a whole. We have replaced it with many faiths and varied makeshift standards that make our life a chaos. Because these various gods and their demands do not agree with each other and we do not know whom to follow, we are confused and divided against ourselves. In spite of this obvious confusion, or perhaps even because of it, there is today everywhere a great deal of talk about preserving Christian values and our Christian civilization.

In present-day America it is no longer stylish to be an "atheist" or even an "agnostic." To admit that you do not believe in God or that you are not sure you believe in Christianity stamps you almost as a subversive and an enemy of the nation. Defenders of the faith spring up everywhere and in some very unexpected places. Among politicians, businessmen, and educators it has become fashionable to be religious. But in view of the obvious confusion of values and faiths we should ask what this "religion" is which is being sold so aggressively in our time? Does this emphasis upon religion and Christian values mean that we really want to take the Christian life seriously and in all earnestness follow the leadership of Jesus Christ? Or is this emphasis upon religion merely an effort to hide the deep uncertainty concerning all moral values that threatens and frightens us?

In order to give a meaningful answer to this question it is necessary to examine the nature of the Christian life. What is this Christianity everybody is advocating nowadays? Has it any relationship or similarity to the historical faith of the church and the witness of the Bible? What is the Christian answer to the problem of moral standards? In what way is the Christian life different from the life advocated by those who do not believe in Christianity? And we must not deceive ourselves. In spite of the new popularity of Christianity there are many other religions to be found in America. These religions which compete with the Christian faith are not necessarily openly known as religions. It isn't Shintoism or Buddhism or Mohammedanism that is capturing the imagination of modern man in the West. But religious alternatives to Christianity exist. Naturalism is one such alternative. Its god is nature, its creed is that nature can do no wrong, and its ethical standard is that whatever is natural is good. Relativism is another such religion. Its god is man, and its ethical standard is that whatever man thinks is good actually is good because he thinks so. And there are many other ways of life that are offered to us as alternatives to the Christian way.

We must ask ourselves, "What makes a life Christian?" Is the Christian life the same as the happy life, the well-adjusted life, the normal life? What are the characteristics, the distinctive features of the Christian moral structure? Is Christianity the same as "Americanism," and is the Christian life the same as the "American way of life"?

In the following pages an effort has been made to look at the Christian life and to come to a clearer understanding of its meaning. This is an attempt to see the Christian life in contrast to other possible ways to organize life in a meaningful manner. We want to look at all the alternatives, those that are clearly outside of Christianity as well as those alternatives to the Christian life which have infiltrated so deeply that they themselves go under the name of Christianity. All evidence indicates that modern man will have to choose a faith by which to live. The present chaos seems to be the preparation for this choice. Whatever our eventual choice might be, the study of the alternatives offered to Christianity should make ours a more intelligent decision.

PART I

THE LIFE OF MAN UNDER THE LAW

LIFE AS DECISION

One of the oldest arguments among philosophers, psychologists, and theologians deals with the problem of human freedom. Is man free to choose the good life? Is he "the master of his fate and the captain of his soul"? Or has he been shaped by forces beyond his control to be what he is? Into this argument we should like to inject a very self-contradictory and paradoxical statement, namely that man's freedom is his bondage. Man may indeed be free to make any number of important decisions about his life. He may have something to say about the choice of his job, his spouse, his friends, or the kind of life he wants to lead. But there is one choice he cannot make: he cannot choose not to choose. He cannot escape his freedom. He is bound to be free. Whether he likes it or not, whether he believes in it or not, he must live a life of constant and unavoidable decisions.

Let me illustrate. It is night. A man is in a boat that is slowly drifting toward a roaring waterfall. This man, who is wide awake in his boat, cannot escape making a choice. It is true that all his choices may be ultimately meaningless. He may start rowing madly and still be carried by the current across the brink to his destruction. He may do nothing at all and the current may wedge him against a rock and keep him safely until daybreak. Yet this man does not know which is the proper decision. And he realizes that not to do anything is also a decision. The current is carrying his boat whether he likes it or not. He cannot ask for time out while he makes up his mind as to the possible alternatives. There he sits in his boat, and everything he does or does not do is committing him. Not to make a decision is also a decision. He cannot escape his freedom; he is bound to be free.

Every man—you and I—is such a person in a boat on the stream of time. The stream keeps on moving. There is nothing we can do about it. We cannot make it stop. In fact, we experience this "time," which we measure so neatly in seconds and minutes, in hours and days, in months and years, in far less comfortable fashion. We all know that time is experienced as "relative," not "absolute"; a minute sitting on a hot stove seems longer than an hour on a davenport with an attractive member of the opposite sex. This relativity of time, some aspects of which can actually be measured, makes our trip on the stream of time even more uncomfortable. Among other things the speed of time seems to accelerate as we grow older. The older we get, the faster it goes, and the time from November 30 to December 25, which seems an eternity when you are six, seems unbelievably shorter when you are thirty. We notice also that old people have a tendency to think of all past time as "only yesterday" or "the other day." This acceleration that makes the river of time flow more and more swiftly is particularly uncomfortable because it gives us less time in which to make our decisions.

Life does not merely demand decision; life *is* decision. The very act of staying alive involves daily decision, and even committing suicide involves decision. Man cannot escape decision. He cannot escape his freedom.

But now the important question arises. Is there anything that can possibly guide us in these decisions that have to be made every day, every hour, every minute of our lives? Is there some standard by which the value of these decisions, their "goodness" or "badness," can be measured? If we want to know the distance from our house to the street, there is a fairly simple way to find out. We can take a tape-measure and measure it. Then we know exactly how far it is. We know it in feet and inches, and if we want to be very scientific we can find out in meters and centimeters, and millimeters. The distance so established is then beyond dispute; anybody else who doubts our word can take the same measuring devices and find out for himself. The standard we are using is the measuring tape which has been divided into units on which we have all agreed. It seems to be an absolute standard and its results seem beyond dispute.

Similarly, we can establish the weight of a car, the speed of an airplane, and many other facts. We have standards, the pound or the gram, the mile per hour or the kilometer per hour; with the help of these standards and with generally accepted measuring devices, the facts we seek can be accurately established.

But how about the decisions we have to make every minute of our lives? Is there any standard by which they can be accurately measured? For example, can you give reasons for your decision to read these pages? Why are you reading an introduction to ethics rather than a detective story? Why are you reading instead of going to the movies or looking at television? How did you arrive at this decision? Was there some standard of importance which you used for your guidance? Similarly, when you choose one person for a friend instead of another, is your decision guided by some standard of attractiveness?

I think few of us would say that we make these decisions purely by chance, as the result of "accident." We would rather say that we have certain standards of what is important and what is unimportant, what is attractive and what is unattractive, what is right and what is wrong. But what kind of standards are they? Can they stand the light of sober and exact examination?

If some are still quite confused about this discussion of our standards for decision, let me give another illustration. The skin of a man—let us call him A—is being penetrated by the knife held by a man whom we shall call B. The result is the death of A. It would be possible to describe this simple event physiologically, from the point of view of A or B. It could be described physically, from the point of view of the force expended and the calories used up by B. There are many ways of scientifically describing what occurred. But in order that we might know whether the action of B upon A is murder, or let us say, an unsuccessful operation, we must make a thorough investigation of the motives of B. In other words, we have to deal with the decisions that led him to his action, and apply some kind of standard to his decision.

The difference between a good action and an evil action seems to depend almost entirely upon the motives guiding the decision of the acting person, rather than upon any description, scientific or otherwise, of the action itself.

The great confusion of our age seems to have its origin in our ability to describe scientifically almost any process that occurs and in our inability to understand the personal reasons that underlie all our actions. We see all about us people who make decisions, but we have a difficult time finding some way to measure the value of the decisions they make.

In the most important area of our life, where we are daily engaged in decisions, we are singularly unable to discover any clear-cut rules or standards that could be compared with the objective rules and standards that govern the behavior of the elements in the physical universe. We have a law of gravity which works rather predictably, but we have difficulty discovering a similarly reliable law in the realm of decision. What are we supposed to do?

At this point some people throw up their hands in horror and say, "Let's not do anything. The situation is hopeless. There is no answer to the problem. Let's ignore it; let's keep on living and ask no embarrassing questions about the motives and the decisions involved in our living."

Some people get very angry when an attempt is made to question them about their motives. Even pacifists develop an amazing amount of fighting spirit when their motives and ethical standards are called in question. There is nobody who likes to be questioned about those matters which he considers self-evident to all men of good will, which generally means all men who happen to agree with him. The Greek philosopher Socrates found out that nice, open-minded people like his Athenian countrymen, when questioned persistently enough about their basic assumptions, would not hesitate to kill the questioner. This should be a warning to us. This is a touchy subject. It is always dangerous to ask questions even of ourselves in that realm of life which is cluttered up with prejudices and superstitions we have held so long that their very age has given them authority.

And yet, if we want to push forward to a clearer understanding of the Christian life, we shall have to look for it in the midst of life, and always against the background of other attempts to understand the meaning of life.

We must always keep in mind that standards used to evaluate decision are based upon commitment to some basic source of value. We shall see that there is a great deal of disagreement as to the nature of this basic source. Some see it in man, some in nature, some in the dialectical process, some in the principle of the survival of the fittest, some in truth. Some call it God. We shall find that the character of the standards will vary greatly according to the nature of this basic source, or "god." But in every case we deal with an initial commitment. Of course, there are people in our time who believe that they can take their position outside this stream of life and be uncommitted observers. But it seems obvious that to take this position is also the result of a decision made on the basis of a standard of evaluation. Nobody can escape this fundamental commitment.

What is the commitment that underlies our present investigation? It would indeed be foolish to claim the necessity for commitment and then proceed as if the necessity applied only to others and not to ourselves. Our investigation of the Christian life is based upon the commitment to Jesus Christ as the absolute standard for decision. The concrete meaning of this commitment to the person of Jesus Christ should become clearer in the course of our discussion.

The Christian life as the answer to man's search for a standard for decision is meaningful only if we take time to probe the question deeply and thoroughly. The Christian life as an answer to man's search for a meaningful life is worthless to the man who has never searched. The Christian life is a cure for the disease of meaninglessness, but in order to appreciate the cure —in order that we may be willing to take the medicine —it is essential for us to recognize our disease. It seems, in fact, that one of the great problems facing Christianity in our age is that Christianity offers a radical cure to people who do not even believe they are sick. Small wonder that they have little use for the cure!

Nothing is more worthless than the answer to a question that has never been asked. In order to make the answer count we shall have to ask the question carefully and conscientiously. The question we shall have to ask will center on the subject of ethics. What is right and what is wrong? Are there standards for the decisions that man must make—or are his decisions equally meaningless and his life a huge cosmic joke in which finally all is vanity?

Pre-Ethical Stages

At this point it may be necessary to remind ourselves that wherever people have lived they have differentiated between right and wrong, between good and bad. There isn't a language that lacks words for both "right" and "wrong." There isn't a people which does not distinguish between that which is approved and that which is disapproved. The most primitive as well as the most civilized man judges decisions and groups them into "good" and "bad" decisions. However, we should realize also that there is nevertheless such a thing as pre-ethical behavior. In certain borderline cases of human existence it is possible to act without any clear sense of the meaning of the decisions we make.

After the manner of Emil Brunner, I should like to call one of these pre-ethical stages the stage of immediacy. It is the stage of behavior wherein our actions seem not to be guided by any kind of premeditation or prudential concern, but wherein we do what comes naturally. A small infant, a week or two old, acts and makes decisions. But they are not decisions, properly speaking. When a baby cries or smiles, the action is not the result of some intellectual decision, but is an immediate reflex to some stimulus. Crying and smiling in a baby do not constitute "bad" or "good" action, and we cannot properly call this ethical action.

Similarly, the actions of a very old and senile person are often on the level of immediacy. Here too there seems to be no conscious or even clearly subconscious intellectual process; rather we are dealing with simple responses to simple stimuli. Here we are confronted with the very borderline of the ethical life or the life of decision. Any person who acts genuinely on this level of immediacy is not an ethical person in the strict sense of the word. Mere reaction to a stimulus is not ethical action because it is action that does not involve decision. If I close my eyes when a piece of cinder has gotten into one, I am not doing anything which is morally good or bad. I am merely reacting to a stimulus. If I duck when a hard object is thrown in my direction I am engaged in a similar "reaction." My behavior in such situations may indicate the condition of my reflexes, but it certainly tells nothing about my ethical standards. People who in all situations act within the framework of immediacy are not properly subjects for the student of ethics.

However, a word of warning is in order. There have been philosophical systems and teachers that have proclaimed this stage of immediacy as the ideal stage of human life and attempted to teach man to live constantly on this particular level. In many "back to nature" movements there is a conscious effort to establish artificially a standard of behavior which is found naturally on the stage of immediacy. But such an artificial attempt to be what we are not with the help of a conscious and laborious intellectual decision has nothing to do with the stage of immediacy as we have described it so far. To be a baby is quite different from acting like a baby when one is a man. The important thing about the stage of immediacy is that it is not willed, it is not the result of our decision to live on this level, but it simply is. In this stage a person exists unaware of the level of decision. It is impossible to will oneself without will. It is equally impossible to decide to live without decision.

These artifical attempts to return to a stage of existence we have outgrown are pathetic efforts of our age to escape the rigors of decision. They are significant reflections on the character of our time. We should ruthlessly reveal them for what they are: attempts to flee from being what we cannot help being, attempts to escape our responsibility as human beings.

But before we dismiss this stage of immediacy as a stage we have outgrown and with which we are no longer concerned, we should remind ourselves that there are many decisions every day which we make on no higher level than this level of immediacy. All of us, in a sense, continue with part of our being in the sub-human stage of immediacy.

The second stage of human behavior which may also be described as pre-ethical is the stage of custom. Many people make almost all their so-called decisions not as the result of any intelligent effort, but merely in an attempt to conform to the prevailing custom. In many societies and among numberless people of our own society the question is not, "Is this action good or bad?" or "Is this decision right or wrong?" but, "Is this what everybody else does?" Much of what goes under the name of good could be more aptly described as being the customary thing in our particular society. There is a certain amount of decision involved here, namely the decision to obey or disobey custom. This decision, however, is not on a high level, since we do not evaluate customs but accept them without serious question.

To obey custom, is, of course, often very useful and intelligent. In many instances custom is the accumulated good sense and experience of our social group, and he who obeys custom often benefits unconsciously from the insights of his ancestors. It would be foolish indeed to reject all custom merely because it has been uncritically accepted in other times. Its acceptance or rejection by others should not in any way validate or invalidate the commandments of custom. However, one of the basic weaknesses of acting on the level of custom, from the point of view of the Christian life, is that frequently very important matters and utterly unimportant matters are equally customary. Custom itself does not supply us with the standards which would enable us to distinguish between that which is on the periphery of life and that which is truly essential.

In certain parts of America it is customary to go to church on Sunday. Everybody who is anybody goes to church. Otherwise, however, the life of the community does not indicate that the love of Christ is a dominating influence. Church-going has become a social custom rather than the worship of the living Christ. Yet in the minds of people who operate on the level of custom, obedience to the custom of church-going is identified with the Christian faith. Thus a matter on the periphery of the Christian life becomes the standard by which the health of this life is measured. As a result we frequently live in a fool's paradise because we mistake obedience to custom for the Christian life.

A similar situation prevails in the political realm. Certain assertions about man's freedom and equality are customary in this country. Without any reflection most Americans will assert that they believe men to be equal and free. However, such an assertion is with many people not the result of any personal decision or conviction but merely the repetition of accepted phrases dictated by custom. Whenever we attempt to measure the health of our democracy merely by the number of people who will render the customary lip-service to democratic phrases, we are confusing custom with personal decision, and our evaluation will be most inaccurate.

Since so much of our everyday morality is not the result of ethical decision but merely imitation of behavior observed in others, we live a great deal of our moral life on a pre-ethical stage. We must realize that all of us continue on this stage of custom even though we may have consciously attempted to take the Christian life seriously.

There are numerous striking illustrations of the power of custom in the life of the Christian. For example, most Protestants after attending services in a Roman Catholic church will claim they did not like the service. When we attempt to get to the root of this dislike, those of us who have some theological concern are usually seriously disappointed. Usually the main objections to the Roman Catholic service are the use of Latin, the kneeling, the vestments, the incense, or the acolytes. Some or all of these practices may be contrary to our customs, yet they are on the periphery of theology. Suppose that a Roman Catholic priest, dressed in the proper vestments of our particular group, spoke from the pulpit of one of our churches and extolled salvation by works and the necessity of our co-operation in our salvation. Most of our people would feel less shocked than if they would hear a thoroughly evangelical sermon on salvation by grace alone from a preacher who would then proceed to use an incense pot.

This may help us to understand how much of our daily life, even within the church, is lived on the level of custom. In a study of the Christian life one must constantly inquire as to whether we are speaking about the Gospel of Christ or about the customs and mores of our social group. Frequently, and especially in the field of ethics, the moral customs of our social group have become completely confused with the gospel of the Lord Jesus Christ. We say "Christian behavior" and often mean the behavior of middle-class, white Americans. We forget that our Lord Jesus Christ himself questioned and overthrew some of the most cherished customs of his time.

The Christ who ate with Quislings and prostitutes, who broke the religious laws guarding the Sabbath, is, if taken seriously, a dangerous enemy of all our customs and moral prejudices. Before him our actions cannot be defended by merely appealing to precedent. From this point of view it becomes clear that like the stage of immediacy, the stage of custom is a pre-ethical stage.

Prudential Ethics

Ethics as the intelligent effort to discover standards for decision begins when individual men start to reflect on their concepts of right and wrong. People are constantly making moral judgments in connection with the activities of their everyday life. Sooner or later they may ask themselves, "Why do I consider this action right and this other action wrong? What personal values make me decide in this manner?" Whenever this question is asked personally and seriously, the level of custom has been passed. No longer is action merely an attempt to conform to existing standards which are unhesitatingly accepted. Action is now the result of reflection on the basis of conscious standards of value.

In most efforts to discover a meaningful basis for life the fundamental question is, "What am I living for?" The answer to this question determines the character of our ethics. An ethical system can be called *prudential* if its basic standards are selected with an eye to the future. The goodness or badness of an action depends here on the good or bad end which it is expected to bring about. It measures all decisions by the consequences which may be expected to result. There are several types of prudential ethics.

Hedonism. A hedonist is a person whose supreme standard for ethics is pleasure. He believes that the goodness of an action depends entirely on the amount of pleasure it is going to secure. The good is identified with that which gives pleasure, and evil is identified with that which gives pain.

The difficulty with this system is apparent. Pleasure is the kind of word that means a million things to a million people. What is one man's pleasure is another man's pain. Some people derive pleasure from being spun around in some little machine in an amusement park until their insides are in a state of utter disorganization. They are even willing to pay money for this doubtful privilege. Others suffer pain even at the thought of being subjected to such treatment. Further, there are people who tell me that reading books and listening to classical music are actually painful to them, activities which give others a great deal of pleasure.

Illustrations of the ambiguity of the concept of pleasure could be easily multiplied. One thing is clear: many people are guided in their personal decisions by the search for pleasure. Whatever this pleasure might be, it is their supreme value of life.

If we try to evaluate the consequences of such an ethical standard for the life of man, it is important to distinguish between two main kinds of hedonism. We call them individualistic and universalistic. The first group, represented by men like Epicurus and Omar Khayyam, says that each individual, in order to achieve a meaningful life, must pursue his own pleasure. It is useless and in fact dangerous to attempt to guess what will give meaning to the lives of others. Therefore our actions should be guided entirely by that which will give pleasure to us as individuals. Any effort to guess what might give happiness to others will only lead to general unhappiness.

We can see an element of truth in this position if we remember all the pathetic efforts through which we have tried to make other people happy. We realize that sometimes those who are constantly trying to "make everybody happy" turn out to be terrible pests and bores. Recognizing the futility of such efforts, the individualistic hedonist gives up all efforts in this direction and advocates a clear-cut and self-seeking quest for happiness.

It is not true that this excludes all service to others. The individualistic hedonist knows that it might give him happiness to do certain things for others. However, he realizes all the time that he is not doing it to make others happy, but because doing things for others makes him happy. The ultimate goal is always his own personal pleasure.

Even if pleasure were a clear-cut and constant concept, which it is not, this would be a very shaky foundation for human life. Such individualism sets every man against every other man and thus disrupts and atomizes human society. Historically, hedonism of this type has been accompanied by agnosticism. If people do not believe in a life after death, if pleasure is the only good, they must avoid anything that could bring them in conflict with others and cause pain. Quite logically the great representatives of individualistic hedonism advocated staying out of politics and public life, and in general keeping away from most people, except a few chosen friends.

From this point of view marriage and the rearing of a family were also frowned upon. Bachelorhood was to be the ideal state, involving the least unpleasure. And it is true that every involvement with people is a potential source of pain. If you have a wife and three children you have five people to worry about; if you are single you have just one.

The individualistic hedonists finally realized that life, even lived alone in isolation against the pain that others can inject into one's life, still consists of more pain than pleasure. Thus, from the point of view of an individualistic hedonist, life is simply not worth living. Thinking along these lines many philosophers of this school advocated suicide and not a few practiced it. If all that makes life worthwhile is the pleasure we can squeeze out of it, and if that life must end in death, it is simply not worth living in the first place. And since most natural deaths are more painful and unpleasant than certain types of suicide, it can easily be demonstrated that from a logical adherence to the principles of individualistic hedonism suicide is advisable. Jesus laid down the law of the spiritual life, "He who finds his life will lose it"; and the individualistic hedonists were not exceptions to this rule.

Universalistic hedonists (J. S. Mill, Bentham, Locke, and so forth) work with a different basic assumption. Known also as "utilitarians," their slogan is "the greatest good for the greatest number." Here all people are included in the search for pleasure. If my own pleasure conflicts with the pleasure of the group, I must be willing to sacrifice my personal pleasure for the greater pleasure of the majority.

This system has obvious advantages as an ethical method for the organization of society. It is inclusive and makes it possible to consider not only all the people living today but also the generations that are to come. However, the great difficulty which arises here also is the difficulty of establishing what this "greatest good for the greatest number" in any particular case might be. It is easy to see that communism and Nazism with all their concentration camps and gas chambers might possibly be justified from the point of view of a universalistic hedonist. If six million people are gassed and cremated, what of it? There are two billion people in the world, and if I can convince myself that my action is for the good of this overwhelming majority, my crimes are no longer crimes but are immediately justified.

The greatest good for the greatest number is such a vague principle for ethics that its results in action will depend entirely on the interpretation it receives at any specific time. Advocates of this system, like all others who make pleasure the ultimate good, have difficulty in finding a standard which would enable man to distinguish between various kinds and types of pleasure. The only distinction which a hedonist who wants to be consistent can make is the distinction between more pleasure and less pleasure—a quantitative distinction. At the moment when he attempts to evaluate pleasures qualitatively, claiming that some pleasures are better than others, he is no longer truly a hedonist. He is injecting a different kind of value into his ethics. This has been done by some utilitarians, but it only demonstrates the unsatisfactory character of "pleasure" as the basic value of life.

Before we leave the discussion of hedonism, individualistic and universal, it will be well for us to remind ourselves how many of our actions are in fact guided by a secret hedonism. Even though we may consciously reject hedonism as supplying a valid norm for decision, it is the basis for decision in many of our actions. Although we may not think we should act on this level, we do so in more situations than we like to admit. Even behind our loftiest motives there is often a secret desire for pleasure. Hedonists who are attempting to justify this source of our action may be wrong, but those of us who deny that this source actually exists are equally wrong and in addition less honest.

Christians tend to confuse the Christian life and some form of supernatural hedonism. For, whether you expect your pleasure here on earth or in a life to come, if your actions are guided by your desire for pleasure and your attempts to avoid pain, you are a hedonist, even if pleasure is expected in heaven or pain in hell. A Christian philosophy which is dominated by an attempt to gain pleasures in heaven and avoid the pains of hell is hedonism pure and simple. Even the fact that some church fathers have spent much time and paper in depicting the pleasures of the saints in heaven as they behold the suffering of the damned in hell does not justify such "Christian" hedonism. The main characteristic of all religious hedonism is that it dethrones God and makes the individual's eternal happiness the true good of his life. God becomes then a means to human ends. We use God and the church to achieve our own happiness. Love for one's neighbor is reduced to a means for the accumulation of merits to bring us into heaven. A substantial part of Christian theology has been dominated by this type of religious hedonism. For many Christians, religion can become the most subtle form of self-seeking, of gaining eternal pleasure and avoiding eternal pain. This form of individualistic hedonism, superficially camouflaged by Christian concepts and ideals, we must also keep in mind as we continue our quest for the Christian life.

Naturalism. If pleasure is an uncertain and evasive standard for decision because it means so many different things to so many different people, the question arises whether it may not be possible to discover somewhere a more objective standard which would be true for all people at all times. Naturalistic ethics proposes that this standard may be found in nature. Man is considered a product of nature; some may call him the highest development in the evolutionary process. This evolutionary process, which has produced all the various forms of life, also supplies us with the standard for evaluating all action. Since it is the purpose of nature that the fit should survive, everything that contributes to the survival of the fittest is good, and everything that hampers this survival and helps the unfit to survive is bad.

The advantage of naturalistic ethics over the vague appeal to pleasure is the relative objectivity of the appeal to survival. But while survival is an understandable and unambiguous concept, the word "fit" has generally meant "strong"; thus are the standards of the jungle advocated as adequate to human behavior. Before we attempt to investigate the practical consequences of this position, we should immediately recognize its hidden assumption. The evolutionary process is assumed to be good. It is the optimistic assumption of most biological naturalists that the fit survive, that somehow the process of natural selection selects the good.

What are the consequences of naturalistic ethics in our everyday life? The first consequence is the rejection of all efforts to protect the weak. The naturalist reasons it is evil to interfere with nature by encouraging the survival of the unfit which nature wants to eliminate. Far from praising people for taking care of the insane, for example, we should condemn our society and those willing to spend time and effort to preserve what nature does not desire to preserve. Only those sick people whose restoration to health might be of some use to society should receive medical care. The others, especially the old, should be destroyed or "liquidated."

Another consequence is that the notion of evolution is applied to race. Certain races are assumed to be on a low evolutionary level. Since every race has a place in the steady and gradual process of evolution, there are some races which are inferior to others, which have not yet reached the evolutionary level which the others have reached. Or they are considered the unfit mutations, dead-end streets of evolution. It is from this point of view that the idea of "master-races" and "slave-races" becomes understandable. And we can also see why the treatment of the "slave-races" by the "master-races" is so terrible from a Christian point of view. It is supposed to be "natural." There is no sympathy for frogs among snakes or for flies among frogs. The stronger feeds on the weaker. Such behavior is natural, and, according to naturalistic ethics, provides the proper pattern for human behavior as well.

This naturalistic ethics also finds expression in economics. Here we find those who believe that what is natural is good advocating what has commonly been called "laissez-faire economy." *Caveat emptor,* let the buyer beware, is their slogan. In the economic struggle for survival it is the strong, the fit that should survive. Even if it may not be strictly true that one has to drink a certain kind of whiskey in order to become a man of distinction, business is business, and that is enough justification even for the falsehoods of the advertisements. Indeed, if an advertisement helps a company to survive the struggle for existence, it is a good advertisement—even if it is dangerous and misleading. Efforts to regulate prices, control wages, provide social security and medical care for the improvident constitute interference with the natural economic law, and therefore are evil and bound to lead to disaster. An effort on the part of the government to give people a chance to find employment without respect to their race or color is wrong from the point of view of this naturalistic ethics. For it is alleged that such regulations interfere with freedom—the freedom of the economically strong, of course, the freedom of those who employ or those who control the segregated labor unions which also oppose such regulations. The fact that racial discrimination also interferes with freedom, the freedom of the individual to find a job, is considered irrelevant from the point of view of such a naturalism.

In all ages naturalistic ethics has found a number of eloquent spokesmen. The Sophist Thrasymachus in Socrates' time advocated it, as did Machiavelli two thousand years later. In modern times the most open advocate of naturalism in ethics was the German philosopher Friedrich Nietzsche. He said, for example, "Exploitation does not belong to a depraved or imperfect and primitive society, it belongs to the nature of the living being as a primary organic function; it is a consequence of the intrinsic Will to Power, which is precisely the Will to Life." [1] And he advocated a master-morality against the prevalent slave-morality of Christianity. Harshness, selfishness, aggressiveness are here the true virtues; love, pity and humility appear as vices. On English and American soil Nietzsche has always been most unpopular because of the logical and cold-blooded manner in which he presented his naturalism. Anglo-Saxon naturalism has always been far more cautious, circumspect, and dishonest. But Herbert Spencer, Julian Huxley, and many others, are to be numbered among the biological naturalists.

[1] Friedrich Nietzsche, *The Philosophy of Nietzsche* (New York: Modern Library, 1927), p. 578.

In recent years we have seen naturalistic ethics in action in Nazi Germany. The destruction of the mentally ill and the sterilization of those who were considered biologically unfit to propagate the species were good examples of this type of ethics in action. Just as the naturalistic ethics of Nazism treated man as an animal, so does that of communism. The dialectical process is considered the natural process and the Communist party is the organization which attempts to help this natural process along. Here too, people are merely means to the evolutionary end, and all values are allegedly taken from nature itself.

In America also, voices are heard advocating the ethics of naturalism. Some of the loudest opponents of communism agree with Stalin that we must take our ethics from nature. While "nature" according to the Communists is the "dialectical process," it is, according to others a return to the days of an untrammeled and natural laissez-faire capitalism. The economic "laws of nature" are good, they say, and no men or organization of men shall interfere with them unless they desire to invite disaster. All ethical naturalists agree that what is according to nature is good, although they disagree about the nature of nature.

From our point of view as Christians, a word of caution is in order. Many times in history Christian ethics has had a tinge of naturalism. In their quest for the Christian life, Christians have often attempted to identify the *status quo*, the natural state of things, with the will of God. Especially when "Christian" people of the world have had power, they have tended to substitute power for right. Some of the most eloquent spokesmen of naturalistic power ethics have been men of the cloth. The idol of Machiavelli, because of his absolutely ruthless devotion to power, was Pope Alexander VI. Richelieu, the all-powerful statesman under Louis XIII of France, was a cardinal of the Roman Church. The conquerors of North America used their knowledge of the Old Testament to justify their ruthless treatment of the native Indian population. They identified themselves with the Israelites and the Indians with the Canaanites, whom God had given into their hands for utter destruction. Shem, Ham, and Japheth have been used by Christian theologians to justify slavery, and the New Testament by others to justify anti-Semitism.

Today, many Christians both here and abroad, perfectly satisfied with their naturalistic ethics, attempt to cover it with only a thin veil of pious platitudes. The ethics of naturalism is not merely the enemy outside the gate of the Christian church. It has been comfortable as a parasite in the very center of Christendom. The quest for the Christian life must not overlook the dangers that threaten Christianity from the Christians who have accepted naturalistic ethics, identifying what is with what ought to be.

Relativism. The difficulty of establishing an intelligible ethical standard that is acceptable to everybody should by now be obvious. Concepts like pleasure or nature, though not equally ambiguous, still have a multitude of meanings. It is because of this obvious difficulty that the ethical relativists claim that it is useless to attempt to discover a meaningful standard for ethical behavior. It is impossible, they say, to find a method which would enable us to discover whether any particular decision is right or wrong. There is no experimental approach to ethics, for every situation is unique. In one particular situation we may have the choice between saving someone's life or telling the truth. But what may be right in this one situation may be hopelessly wrong in another. It is impossible to experiment, since identical situations cannot be produced.

In view of these difficulties the ethical relativists suggest with Protagoras, a Greek Sophist, that "man is the measure of all things." One opinion is as good as the next, and everybody has to establish his own ethical standards which then will be true for him and nobody else. In other words, right is what I think is right and wrong is what I think is wrong. There are as many "ethics" as there are people, and there is no way of judging objectively which of all these systems is more right than any other.

This approach is extremely popular in our time and has the advantage of being considered scholarly and objective. It is held by all those who claim that they are trying to be impartial and unprejudiced. Vilfredo Pareto in his work *Mind and Society* says, "The term 'ought' does not correspond to any concrete reality." [2] And in another place, "To say that 'injustice,' whether done to one person or to many, involves an equal offense against justice, is to say a thing that has no meaning. There is no such person as 'Justice' and one cannot imagine what offenses could be offered her." [3] This is an illustration of the attempt of ethical relativists to debunk all values as meaningless and irrelevant. The terms good or bad, right or wrong, are meaningless, and the scholar is expected to operate without them. Value judgments on the part of the historian, sociologist, psychologist, or philosopher make him suspect among his fraternity and definitely "unscientific." If a sociologist such as P. A. Sorokin offends against this code, he is ostracized and called a charlatan—even if he happens to be the head of the sociology department of Harvard University.

It is important for us to dwell for a moment on this aspect of relativistic ethics, for students are being trained today to accept ethical relativism as the infallible dogma. The self-contradiction involved in this teaching is obvious. On behalf of open-mindedness we are confronted by people with utterly closed minds who dogmatically assert the absolute truth that there is no absolute truth.

Again, it is of importance to realize that the Christian church has not been immune to ethical relativism.

[2] Charles H. Patterson, *Moral Standards* (New York: Ronald Press, 1949), p. 59.
[3] Ibid., p. 60.

That "man is the measure of all things" expressed in religious terms has meant that there is no religious truth or falsehood, that all religions are equally good if held by sincere people. It does not matter what you believe; all you need is some kind of belief—prohibition, the cross, pacifism, they are all the same. There is no such thing as heterodoxy, for everybody who is sincere is also orthodox. In popular parlance this means "we are all going to the same place," even if some think it is nirvana, heaven, hell, purgatory, or the millennium.

For the ethical relativists, there is one exception to this rule in religion. The person who insists that there is truth and therefore that there is also falsehood, that there is good and therefore also evil, the person who insists that it makes a difference what you believe, is considered "intolerant."

Here too, heterodoxy, every man being his own infallible pope and inspired Scripture, has become orthodoxy; and people who do not conform to orthodox heterodoxy because of their heterodox orthodoxy risk their acceptance within the elect circle of the tolerant and open-minded. Again we see that ethical relativism affects Christendom as well as every other part of our society. As Christians do not live in isolation, the patterns of thought which dominate our culture never fail to influence the Christian church.

Aesthetic Ethics

While prudential ethics is always directed towards the future, there are other efforts to make life meaningful here and now without regard to anything that the future might bring or take away. The person who believes in any kind of prudential ethics sees every act justified by what its results in the future might be. It is the result of the act which makes it good or bad, rather than the act itself. For example, the murders which the Nazis committed in their concentration camps were considered "good" by many sincere Nazis because they were supposed to result in the triumph of a biologically superior race over biologically inferior races. Similarly but in ecclesiastical garb, the Bishop of Verden said in 1411, "When the existence of the church is threatened, she is released from the commandments of morality. With unity as the end, the use of every means is sanctified, even cunning, treachery, violence, simony, prison, death. For all order is for the sake of the community, and the individual must be sacrificed for the common good." The person committed to such an ethical system might very possibly spend his entire life doing unpleasant things, or even evil things, for the sake of some good that is believed to be the eventual result. This good may in fact never be attained. The good is always in the future and the present evil is merely a passing means to achieve the good.

We all know people who all their life do work which they don't really like but which is profitable, in order that at the end they might for a while do things they like. The trouble is that often such a person retires at 65 to do what he wants to do, and then dies at 66.

For fifty years he did things that seemed boring or perhaps even evil to him so that he might do the pleasant and the good for only a few months.

Because of this disappointing aspect of the prudential approach to life, some suggest a different way. Forget the past and the future, they say. Live now! What use is it to work for future pleasures or worry about future pains? And why worry about nature? Nature does not worry about you. Try to make your life meaningful, even though it is ultimately meaningless. Try to enjoy your life, even though pain may outweigh pleasure. And if there is to be pain, perhaps you can learn to enjoy even pain. Don't attempt to give to the universe a meaning which it does not have. Do not try to find a purpose for your life that lies in the future. Face the hopelessness of your situation and then try to make the best of it.

Bertrand Russell writes, "Brief and powerless is man's life; on him and all his race the slow, sure doom falls pitiless and dark. Blind to good and evil, reckless of destruction, omnipotent matter rolls on its relentless way; for man, condemned today to lose his dearest, tomorrow himself to pass through the gate of darkness, it remains only to cherish ere yet the blow falls, the lofty thoughts that ennoble his little day; disdaining the coward terrors of the slave of fate, to worship at the shrine that his own hands have built; undismayed by the empire of chance, to preserve a mind free from the wanton tyranny that rules his outward life; proudly defiant of the irresistible forces that tolerate, for a moment, his knowledge and his condemnation, to sustain alone, a weary but unyielding Atlas, the world that his own ideals have fashioned despite the trampling march of unconscious power." [4]

In spite of the apparent hopelessness of man's situation, it is good to make the most sense out of it that we can—even though life does not really have any absolute sense. The sense life has is the sense we are willing to give it. Man defiantly makes sense out of life which really is only a part of a completely senseless universe. In other words, although there is no purpose to life or love or suffering, though death is the end of everything, men can attempt to use their short day to give their own meaning to life while it lasts. The meaning of life is not in the future but here and now.

We call this type of ethics "aesthetic ethics" because our senses and emotions are used to give meaning to life and to transform meaninglessness into beauty. Perhaps the most brilliant attempt at aesthetic transformation can be found in Greek tragedy. Here life is transformed poetically. Beholding a Greek tragedy, we can appreciate the meaninglessness of life. We are personally enriched and perhaps even purified, although there is no happy end, although life is just as meaningless as it has ever been. Somehow we have seen suffering become beautiful.

Greek drama is a supreme effort to defy the chaotic universe and, by representing it beautifully, to make

---

[4] Bertrand Russell, *Selected Papers of Bertrand Russell* (New York: Modern Library, 1927, pp. 14 f.

it meaningful and transparent. In *Trojan Women* by Euripides we see the Greeks kill the infant son of the Trojan hero Hector because he might otherwise revenge the defeat and destruction of Troy. Even as they kill him, they know that this is a horrible and meaningless crime. The poet makes the horrible aesthetically beautiful. Even the horror of war, of slavery, of sickness, of death, can be made meaningful to man because the artist can make it beautiful. In painting, in sculpture, and in poetry, suffering becomes beautiful and the meaninglessness of life receives aesthetic meaning. Perhaps a quotation from Søren Kierkegaard's *Either/Or* will help us to understand the meaning of aesthetic ethics. He says: "What is a poet? A poet is an unhappy being whose heart is torn by secret sufferings, but whose lips are so strangely formed that when the sighs and the cries escape them, they sound like beautiful music. His fate is like that of the unfortunate victims whom the tyrant Phalaris imprisoned in a brazen bull and slowly tortured over a steady fire; their cries could not reach the tyrant's ears so as to strike terror into his heart; when they reached his ears they sounded like sweet music." [5]

Before we look at two types of aesthetic ethics a little more closely, we must again remind ourselves that Christianity can be robbed of its ultimate meaning if it is given the aesthetic treatment. When we think of some of our hymns and some of our paintings, we can

[5] Robert Bretall, *A Kierkegaard Anthology* (Princeton, N. J.: Princeton University Press, 1947), p. xxvi.

see that we Christians attempt to escape the horror of decision for or against the crucified Son of God by transforming his suffering aesthetically and making him into something else than the man of sorrows, the suffering servant of Isaiah. Remember Isaiah 53:2, 3:

"He had no form or comeliness that we should look at him,

and no beauty that we should desire him.

He was despised and rejected by men;

a man of sorrows, and acquainted with grief;

and as one from whom men hide their faces

he was despised, and we esteemed him not." [6]

Compare this with your own favorite picture of Jesus, and ask yourself, am I engaged in aesthetic escape from decision? Do I want a different alternative from "Christ crucified" or "meaninglessness"? By and large we do want a different alternative. Christendom has always been in danger of escaping from the discipleship of the living Christ into the worship of some beautiful saviour.

But now some brief words about two specific types of aesthetic ethics. Aesthetic ethics may be concerned with being, the person or personality and its development; or it may be concerned with existence, action, and decision. For the sake of classification we shall call the former the *ethics of self-realization*. Here the good is that which helps to bring about the most complete development of the personality. The "self" is not

---

[6] Biblical quotations unless otherwise indicated are from the Revised Standard Version.

only the body but also the mind; it includes also our friends, associates, and all the things and events about us which make us what we are. The more I understand of this being as it touches my personality, the greater is my self. It is my ethical task to enlarge and integrate my self as far as possible. The more I know, the greater becomes my self and the more meaningful becomes my life. The goal of the ethics of self-realization is the development of personality; that is, a more inclusive personality which exists in harmony with all other personalities. The individual must lose himself in the universal self. The question as to the ultimate meaning of life and personality is ignored.

A different kind of aesthetic ethics is suggested by modern atheistic _existentialism_. This movement emphasizes man's freedom and responsibility and has found its most famous spokesman in the Frenchman, Jean Paul Sartre. Though existentialists would protest loudly if classified among those advocating an aesthetic ethics, such a classification seems justifiable for a number of reasons.

Existentialists do not believe that their actions have any ultimate meaning, because life itself has no ultimate meaning. As Simone de Beauvoir puts it, "Man fulfills himself within the transitory or not at all." [7] In other words, our actions must have meaning for us right now; there is no other place, heaven or hell, after the revolu-

---

[7] Simone de Beauvoir, _The Ethics of Ambiguity_ (New York: Philosophical Library, 1948), p. 127.

tion or after the world-wide acceptance of free enterprise, when all is going to be well.

People who believe in a future in which all difficulties disappear can justify their troubles and sacrifices as means to this glorious future. Existentialism denies such a future altogether. There is no goal in life except the life as it is lived now. Madame de Beauvoir says, "If division and violence define war, the world has always been at war and always will be; if man is waiting for universal peace in order to establish his existence validly, he will wait indefinitely: there will never be any other future." [8] The good is action, the assertion of human freedom over everything that tries to thwart it. The ethical life is "to will freedom" for oneself and all other men. It is in living to the fullest that we live best. Decision and action are self-justifying. Madame Beauvoir says further, "Any man who has known real loves, real revolts, real desires, and real will knows quite well that he has no need of any outside guarantee to be sure of his goals; their certitude comes from his own drive. There is a very old saying which goes, 'Do what you must come what may.' That amounts to saying in a different way that the result is not external to the good will which fulfills itself in aiming at it. If it came to be that each man did what he must, existence would be saved in each one without there being any need of dreaming of a paradise where all would be reconciled in death." [9] Right and wrong depend not upon man-

[8] Ibid., p. 119.
[9] Ibid., p. 159.

kind, but upon the individual man who alone makes anything right or wrong. Right is to act; wrong is to vegetate.

Before we leave the ethics of self-realization and of existentialism we must again remind ourselves that these ideas can be found also within Christendom. There are many so-called Christians who discard the ultimate truth of Christianity and use it merely as a means to a fuller life. They need peace of mind or peace of soul; they want to stop worrying and start living here and now. They are not concerned about the future, but Christianity seems to them a way to live the aesthetically valid life now. Their alleged Christianity expresses itself in a love for hymns, especially Christmas carols, although they do not believe in the Christ. It expresses itself in love for dimly illuminated Gothic churches which create an aesthetically satisfying atmosphere. The ultimate truth of Christ does not concern them. Christianity is merely a psychological crutch.

Similarly there are those who dissolve the essence of the Christian Gospel by making the church into a means of action for action's sake. They do not want to ask whether Christianity is true; they want to do things. Some of the things they want to do are very praiseworthy—they want to clear slums, build hospitals, rehabilitate drunkards, abolish drunkenness and crime. But in the hustle and bustle of all their activities they never find time to ask why? Why clear slums? Why work for social justice? These questions they ignore.

They flee from decision into action. Activity—any activity—becomes the substitute for responsible decision. As a result they confuse the important and the unimportant and lose all opportunity to live a meaningful Christian life. They are so busy everywhere that they cannot even hear what Christ is trying to say to them in his word.

The ethics of self-realization and of activity for activity's sake can be found in the very heart of Christendom.

Idealistic Ethics

In addition to the proponents of prudential ethics and aesthetic ethics, there are those who seek their standards of right and wrong not in man or nature, not in personality or action, but in an *ideal* outside of man and nature. They propose an idealistic ethics, believing that such an ideal can be discovered and that it is man's task to abide by it. But how can this ideal be discovered? Here opinions differ.

Ethics of Intuition. There are those who believe that all men have an "intuitive" knowledge of right and wrong as part of their very make-up. Just as men have eyes and thus can see, ears and thus can hear, all men have a moral sense which makes it possible for them to tell right from wrong. This moral sense is commonly located in the conscience, but even the advocates of this theory disagree as to the exact content of the conscience. There are some who believe that the conscience tells all men that it is wrong to murder, lie, cheat, steal, or commit adultery, and that it is right to be honest, courteous, courageous, and just. Anyone who denies such an obvious fact, they say, is morally blind.

Certain philosophers have tried to give a more sophisticated description of these rules which we all know by intuition to be right. The English philosopher, Henry Sidgwick, claimed that there are three obvious rules or maxims which we know intuitively to be true and reasonable. The first of the rules he calls the *Maxim of Benevolence*. It says, "I ought not to prefer my own lesser good to the greater good of another." The second maxim, he calls the *Maxim of Prudence*, "A smaller present good is not to be preferred to a greater future good." (Allowance being made for certainty and attainability.) The third maxim is the *Maxim of Justice*, "What I judge to be right must, unless I am in error, be judged to be right by all rational beings who judge truly of the matter."

Even a very superficial examination of these maxims reveals that they are vague and open to any number of interpretations. Even if two people should accept these standards, their interpretation of these general rules would still make their personal standards quite different.

In spite of all the obvious difficulties of "intuitionist ethics," even a philosopher like Henri Bergson believed that there are supraintellectual experiences which are at the basis of the moral judgments of heroes and saints. However, the unreliable character of the human conscience and its varying sensitivity has made the intuitionist's point of view hard to defend. Even if we should grant with intuitionism's critics that such rules of right and wrong which are available to all men through their conscience are hard to establish, it would still not mean that such rules do not exist. There is an important difference between the claim that there is such a thing as right and wrong apart from man's opinions and desires, and the claim of the intuitionist that this knowledge of right and wrong is easily available and can be obtained with the help of the moral sense.

Rationalistic Ethics. Besides intuitionism there is another type of idealistic ethics which claims that the basic standard for right and wrong can be found through the exact use of reason. Perhaps the most famous representative of such a rationalistic ethics was the German philosopher Immanuel Kant. In his famous *Critique of Practical Reason* he suggested that a careful examination of the human mind reveals at the bottom a sense of duty which is the basis for all ethical action. We all have in us a "sense of ought." We all know there is a difference between what we like to do and what we ought to do. Often we know very definitely that we would like to do one thing yet ought to do another; and quite often we will do what we ought to do rather than what we like to do. If there is a fire in a house and we pass by and hear somebody scream inside, we would like to stay out on the sidewalk where it is safe; yet many of us, Christians and pagans, will try to get in and help—not because we want to but because we know we ought to.

Some years ago I hit a man with my car. It was raining hard, the time was one o'clock in the morning, and there wasn't another soul around. My car was not damaged, the man was unconscious, and for all I knew he was killed. My immediate impulse was to get into my car and drive away. That's what I wanted to do; instead I ran to the nearest telephone and called the ambulance and the police, because I knew that this was what I ought to do—and the *ought* was stronger than the *want*.

Kant says that moral law is not a statement of how men do behave, but how they ought to behave. A moral law is always an imperative. We all know an innocent man ought not to be punished for the acts of a guilty man. A man ought not to return evil for good.

It is upon this "sense of ought" which reason can discover and analyze that Kant built his famous "categorical imperative." It reads as follows: "Act in such a manner that the rules governing your action could become the universal law." This is, of course, the Golden Rule in complicated terminology—do unto others as you would have them do unto you.

Kant believed that he had found here the bedrock of a rational ethics. It did not take faith or intuition but only logical thinking to arrive at this position and to realize its soundness.

For us the difficulty remains, what about those people who are willing to let murder or adultery become the universal law? Is their action right because they are willing to let everybody else act in the same manner? Appealing as Kant's ethics is, it does not supply the firm foundation for the good life which he hoped it would.

Again in intuitionism and rationalism we see attempts to find standards for living which have seriously affected Christendom. Many Christians consider that to be right which they intuitively know to be right. These are the people who claim to have a private wire to God and therefore make their ethical decisions not in imitation of Christ but on the basis of their own intuitive insights. In every generation, in every Christian congregation, there are some "enthusiasts" who attempt to lead Christian people on their own inspired path.

Similarly, it is possible to show that rationalism has not failed to influence Christian ethics. Efforts to water down the absolute demands of Christian discipleship are generally based on the claim that ethical laws must be reasonable and that some of the New Testament commands simply do not meet this specification. For example, throughout the Middle Ages theological efforts were made to prove that to love one's neighbor means, first, to love God; second, to love oneself; third, to love people who are by nature close to us, our relatives and friends; and only fourth, all other men. This concept of ordered love was an effort to water down the demands of the Gospel which are "unreasonable" from the point of view of human competence and reason. Again and again sermons are preached in which the attempt is being made to make "love of the enemy" more reasonable—by explaining it away. The Sermon on the Mount is a favorite passage for those who would like to make the Christian way of life more acceptable to human reason. Throughout the history of the Christian church, the influence of rationalistic ethics upon the Christian life may be observed.

Here, as in all other efforts to find standards for the decisions of life, we have discovered that philosophical attempts to undergird ethics have exerted great influence upon the Christian church. It must be clear by now that the Christian life cannot be understood in isolation from man's efforts to give meaning to his decisions. Christianity has always existed in conflict and tension with all other ethical systems. This conflict has not only changed the world but also has influenced the church.

Before we leave the discussion of the philosophical efforts to find standards for the decisions that confront men, it is necessary to point out one basic distinction between all ethical systems. They are all either formulistic or teleological. That is, they are centered either in the motive or in the goal of man's action. A formalistic approach to ethics emphasizes the importance of the intention. A lie is not telling an untruth but rather an attempt to deceive. If I tell you that New York is the capital of the United States, this is not a lie if I honestly believe it to be the case. In order for this statement to be a lie it must be the result of my intention to deceive. Even if I tell you the truth by mistake but intended to tell you a lie, I am really lying, according to formalism.

On the other hand, we may judge actions by their results rather than by their intentions. If I drive my car recklessly, even though I have no intention to kill anybody, I am not absolved from blame in case I do. A doctor who gives a patient a wrong drug by his carelessness is not absolved from blame because he did not intend to do so. Here we see clearly a teleological approach to ethics: it is the result rather than the motive that counts.

Although it is important to distinguish between these two ethical approaches, we should remember that most of us use both approaches simultaneously. Even the courts take into consideration both the motive and the outcome. It is significant, however, that Christianity asserts that in all important ethical decisions the motive is the significant feature. It is the tree which brings forth the fruit. If it is evil none of the results can be good from the point of view of Christian ethics. In this sense Christian ethics is formalistic rather than teleological.

THE RELIGIOUS SEARCH FOR VALUE

We have studied the quest for standards for decision and have seen how it has led men to establish many different goals. Some hoped to give meaning to life by advocating the pursuit of pleasure. Some hoped to find the meaning of our existence in nature and advocated conformity to laws as we observe them day by day. Some saw meaning only in that life which gives up all search for meaning and makes the best of life as it is from day to day. Others hoped to discover the clue to meaningful life and valid standards for decision by intuition or reason.

So far we have examined only the search for value which hopes to find meaning in life without recourse to the source and ground of all life. All the efforts so far discussed have been essentially efforts to discover standards for decision apart from God. We noted briefly the uncertain and ambiguous character of all these standards. Yet, we repeat, man must act. He absolutely needs standards for his unavoidable decisions. Where can he find them? There has always been the answer—in religion.

The religious search for value starts with the acceptance of God as the standard for all decisions. And here we immediately encounter difficulties, for not all religions believe in a God who is good and thus an acceptable source of ethical life. The Greeks, for example, worshiped divine beings who were of little help in man's quest for the meaningful life. The Greek gods possessed every vice and every virtue which man possesses, but to a much higher degree. Zeus, the king of the Greek gods, lied and committed adultery, and so did his associates. The philosopher Plato was so disgusted with this popular Greek theology that he banned the writings of Homer and Hesiod from his ideal state.

Not all religions have supplied their devotees with standards for right and wrong. In fact, in many instances there has been no clear correlation between "religious" and "moral," and a great deal of organized immorality has been carried on in the name of the gods. Yet there have always been some prophets and saints who have protested this identification of the gods with our own desires and vices. Men like Plato felt that there must be a god who is the source of goodness and the standard of goodness. Similarly, the Persian and Hindu and many other great historical religions have attempted to find the standards for the good life among the gods.

But even if it is assumed that a god is good, that he is the standard for right and wrong for men, the question still remains, how can I make this goodness of God real in my life? Granted that my life would have meaning if it were in tune with God, what can I do to accomplish this end? How can I become God-like?

This question has been answered differently by various religions; and sometimes the same religion has given different answers at different times. But the problem has always been the same: granted that God is the absolute standard for a meaningful and moral life, how can I bring my life into conformity with his will? This is the age-old question of the religious search for value. Human answers to this question confront us when we see an Indian fakir on his bed of nails, the ritual dance of an African tribe, or the dusty clouds of a "Holy Roller" meeting. The hermit on his pillar in Egypt and the garbed religious beggar at Grand Central Station in New York, the Mohammedan soldier and the crusader fighting against him, the Christian medical missionary and the African native who kills his twin children—they are all giving their answer to the question, if God is God, what must man do to live the good life?

For the sake of simplicity, we can divide all human answers to this question into three groups. First there are those who believe that they can find the ultimate religious meaning of their lives through discipline of the will. Secondly, there are those who believe that they can find the meaning of life through exercises of the soul. Thirdly, there are those who believe that the ultimate meaning of life can be found through the intellect. These three approaches are commonly known as legalism, mysticism, and rationalism.

Legalism

We all know what "legalistic" religion is. We have it described for us in the New Testament as the religion of the scribes and Pharisees. But it is not found only among the Jews. Among all religious men there are some who attempt to achieve the goal of life by way of the law.

The legalist believes that the will of God has been expressed in the form of commandments or laws which man can and must fulfill. To do good is to live according to these laws. To do evil is to break any of these laws.

We know how important the "Torah," the Law, was to the Jews of Jesus' time. It seemed so important to them that they had added to the laws of the Pentateuch all sorts of explanations and comments which were supposed to make it easier for men to abide by them. They had built, as they said, a fence around the "Torah."

We know for example how they enlarged on the Sabbath law. In Exodus 31:14-15, we read, "You shall keep the sabbath, because it is holy for you; every one who profanes it shall be put to death; whoever does any work on it, that soul shall be cut off from among his people. Six days shall work be done; but the seventh is a sabbath of solemn rest, holy to the Lord; whoever does any work on the sabbath day shall be put to death."

This was one of the covenant laws of God, and man's relationship to God depended upon obedience to this law. For that reason the Jewish rabbis immediately proceeded to lay down interpretations to these laws which were supposed to prevent the breaking of the commandment. For example, an orthodox Jew does not travel on the Sabbath. Even if the journey is distinctly a pleasure trip it is forbidden, since it would constitute a breach of the Sabbath commandment. Similarly, an orthodox Jew does not switch on an electric light on the Sabbath, for even this simple act is considered work and is therefore forbidden. He does not carry anything, even a handkerchief, on the Sabbath, because this too would be work and a breach of the law.

Similar illustrations could be given concerning all the other commandments. The important thing for us to remember is that right and wrong are here determined "legally." Conformity to divine law is right, breaking the divine law is wrong. And this law is a code which is available to all men. For the legalist, the problem "What is right?" does not exist. His main problem is rather that of the accurate observation of the laws which are established as right. It is taken for granted that men can observe these laws. In addition, "religious lawyers" work out systems that make the observation of these laws a little less burdensome. For example, ways have been devised to travel more than the allowed distance on the Sabbath. Similarly, it is possible to carry a handkerchief by tying it around the wrist, where it represents a piece of clothing, and thus avoid the prohibition of the Sabbath law in case a handkerchief is needed.

The Jewish religion of Jesus' time had completely formalized the ethical life. Obedience to a code had taken the place of any real concern for justice and righteousness. Sabbath observance was given more attention than love and mercy, and our Lord was severely criticized for healing the sick on the Sabbath.

But Jewish legalism is only one form of religious legalism. Confucius' teachings, the self-discipline of the Stoics, the ritual observances of the Mohammedans, are all attempts to live the good life by means of obedience to the law. For our study of the Christian life it is of the greatest importance to remember that such legalism can also be found in the Christian church. Not more than a hundred years after St. Paul the Christian church began to be dominated by a spirit which reduced the Gospel into a new law. To be a Christian meant to obey the laws of the church. There were always prophetic voices who protested against this codification of the Christian life, but they proved to be voices crying in the wilderness. Christendom eventually developed a legal system of right and wrong which made it possible to catalog every action as virtuous, indifferent, venial sin or mortal sin. Again the theologians degenerated into lawyers and the great popes of the Middle Ages were almost all brilliant lawyers rather than creative theologians. They knew the law and they knew how to apply it. In their opinion, Christianity was law. The Christian was the person who obeyed this law and if he disobeyed he was informed of the legal steps necessary to correct his failures and pay his fines.

Even though the Reformation was essentially a revolt against this legalistic concept of Christianity, the churches of the Reformation were soon involved in a similar kind of legalism. Furthermore, if we ask the average person today about the meaning of Christianity to him, he will think almost invariably of rules and laws. If you follow these rules and fulfill these laws you are allegedly a Christian; if you don't obey the laws you are not. These rules may deal with your diet on Friday, or the alcoholic content of your beverages on any day of the week. But wherever we find obedience to rules as the criterion of the Christian life, we are dealing with legalism, the attempt to find the ultimate religious significance of life through the will.

Mysticism

There are also those who believe that they can find the ultimate meaning of life through exercises of the soul. In order to live the good life, in order to live in touch with God, they suggest the training of the religious emotions. For them religion and religious value are essentially the domain of feeling rather than of will. Schleiermacher, the famous German theologian of the nineteenth century, described religion as the "feeling of absolute dependence." Thus we can approach God by cultivating our religious feelings.

The two essential features of religious mysticism are first, that it wipes out any clear distinction between God and man, that the best in man and God are identified; second, that there is a method which men can use to emphasize the divine in themselves and thus unite themselves with God.

Again it is possible to find such a mystical search for value in all religions. But it is in the East that mysticism has reached its most complete development. Perhaps an example will help to illustrate this typical self-identification with God which characterizes the mystic. In the Persian mysticism of Rumi Jalaluddin we read as follows:

"I am the dust in the sunlight, I am the ball of the sun, to the dust I say remain and to the sun roll on.

"I am the mist of morning. I am the breath of even. I am the rustling of the grove, the surging wave of the sea.

"I am the mast, the rudder, the steersman and the ship. I am the coral reef on which it founders.

"I am the tree of life and the parrot in its branches, silence, thought, tongue, and voice.

"I am the breath of the flute, the spirit of man, I am the spark in the stone, the gleam of gold in metal.

"The candle and the moth fluttering around it, the rose and the nightingale drunk with its fragrance.

"I am the chain of being, the circle of the spheres, the scale of creation, the rise and the fall.

"I am what is and is not. I am—O Thou who knowest, Jalaluddin, O say it—I am the soul in all." [1]

That the soul and God are the same in the belief of the mystic is further illustrated by the Indian Acharya Sankara. Commenting on the Upanishads he says: "The Atman (soul or god, identified by Sankara) to know whom is salvation, not to know whom is bondage to the world, who is the root of the world, who is the basis of all creation, through whom all exists, through whom all is conceived—the unborn, the deathless, the fearless, the good, without second—He is the Real. He is thy Self. And therefore that art thou." [2] Later, "Finer than the fine yet am I greatest, I am the All in its complete fullness; I the most ancient, the Spirit, the Lord God. The golden-gleaming am I of form divine, without hand and foot, rich in unthinkable might. Sight without eyes, hearing without ears, free from all form I know, but me none knows. For I am Spirit, am Being." [3]

There are many similar statements which show the mystical identification of the soul with God in the religious literature of the East. The road to the good life is essentially a road of introspection. Man becomes good by shaking off the shackles of earth and uniting his soul with the divine. He becomes good not by doing anything for anybody, not by obeying laws that confront him from the outside, but rather he becomes

---

[1] Rudolf Otto, *Mysticism East and West* (New York: Macmillan, 1938), p. 74.
[2] Ibid.
[3] Ibid.

good by losing himself in the Divine All. He withdraws from the world of sense and climbs up to God. And the mystics even suggest a ladder (*scala paradisi*) which he can use to reach God. There are certain practices—all sorts of ascetic rituals, fastings, and floggings—which make it possible for a man's soul to ascend to God. There are also some mystics who suggest alcoholic and grossly sexual orgies to free the soul from the body. Although there are great differences in detail, mysticism insists everywhere that there is a method which man can use to ascend to God.

We have said that the characteristics of the mystical search for value are the lack of a clear distinction between God and man and the use of a method, a mystical ladder to reach God. These characteristics are found in Christian as well as in non-Christian mysticism. A few examples may suffice. Meister Eckhart, a medieval German mystic, said, "God made all things through me, when I had my existence in the unfathomable ground of God." Another mystic, Angelus Silesius, said in his *Cherubic Pilgrim*, "Nothing exists save Thou and I, and if we two were not God would be God no more, the heavens would fall. I am God's other self, in me alone he finds what in eternity will be both like and similar to him."

Even in Christian mysticism the soul and God are identified. And here, too, a number of methods are suggested which are supposed to free the soul from its earthly shackles for union with God. Asceticism, fasting and self-chastisement are some of the ways which are supposed to lead the individual into union with the divine. Christian mystics do not refrain from describing this union with God in utterly sensual and even sexual terms. The nun Mechtild of Magdeburg, for example, who wrote in the thirteenth century, used almost sickeningly sensual terms to describe in detail the soul's union with God.

For our study it is important to note that the mystic always sees the problem of ethics as a purely personal problem of the soul's relationship to God. To the mystics generally the problems of society seem utterly unreal. They are concerned only with the soul's advance towards God. Their personal salvation seems to be the only "good" they know.

It should be obvious that there are many Christians now and in the past whose behavior is determined completely by this ethical pattern of mysticism. They have divorced ethics, the problem of decision, from the society in which they live. The good is for them an emotional intoxication. There are movements within Christendom today which have all the earmarks of such mysticism, providing the basis for Christianity's reputation as an "opiate" of the people. In their preoccupation with the ascent to God they are totally oblivious of the world in which they live.

Mysticism of this type encourages utter political and social irresponsibility. It becomes a welcome tool in the hands of imperialism and political corruption. The religious mysticism which confronts us in our time lacks most of the real and profound spiritual exaltation that can be observed in Meister Eckhart or the great Hindu mystics. But around us we see today a "poor man's mysticism" on the increase, in the enthusiastic cults of holiness and pentecostal worship. Here we can observe the attempt to escape from the harsh realities of life through emotional intoxication, and at the same time an utter lack of responsible social and political participation.

Mysticism is indeed still with us. In our day, as in all ages before us, there are many who attempt to attain the good life by uniting themselves with God through emotional exaltation, and who find their guide for the decisions of life in the realm of feeling.

Rationalism

It is the characteristic belief of the rationalists that "the good" or "God" can be reached by the method of rational thought, by logic and the dialectical process. It is through reason rather than law or feeling that the meaningful life, that is, the good life, can be attained.

Because of this insistence on clear thinking and logic, the rationalistic way to God has never been as popular as the "way of feeling" or even the "way of law." Anyone can get emotionally intoxicated, under the proper guidance; and almost anyone can obey certain laws, if they are simple enough; but not everyone can think straight or even follow a logical argument. It is this fact which has made religious rationalism always the approach of a minority.

Just as the Jews provide an example of legalism and

the Hindus an example of mysticism, so the Greeks may be described as a people particularly dedicated to the road of reason. It was Socrates, the great Greek teacher, who believed that evil is essentially the same as ignorance. This means that people could be freed from evil if they could only be freed from their ignorance. Throughout his life, Socrates attempted to implement this belief by teaching, by asking his contemporaries questions designed to reveal and dispel human ignorance. He believed sincerely that to be bad was bad for you. Reduced to its simplest implications this opinion was the result of the following process of reasoning: the bad man makes the people about him bad. It is bad people, not good people, who harm you. If you make the people about you evil, these people whom you have perverted will in the end harm you. Thus by being bad you hurt yourself in the long run. As Socrates vainly pointed out to his judges in his *Apology,* it is simply not intelligent to make people evil.

To Socrates and other Greek thinkers God was the supreme intellect, the reason, the logos of the universe. It was by becoming reasonable that we were to become God-like; philosophy was the road to goodness. The Greek thinkers believed firmly that virtue could be taught. Plato and Aristotle, though in disagreement on many things, both believed that the existence of God could be rationally demonstrated, and they developed intricate intellectual proofs which were to demonstrate God's existence. Once God's existence was established, the nature of the good life and the necessity of living the good life would follow logically.

The intellectualism of the Greeks found its way into Christianity. Many of the great theologians of the Middle Ages were profoundly influenced by Plato and Aristotle. They accepted the road of reason as a valid road to God. In the second century Justin Martyr said, "Those who live according to reason are Christians, even though they are accounted atheists. Such were Socrates and Heraclitus among the Greeks, and those like them." This notion had been taken up by two great Christian theologians from Alexandria in Egypt, Clement and Origen. This line of thought led the great scholastic theologians Anselm of Canterbury, Peter Abelard and Peter Lombard to construct theological systems based firmly on reason. The development reached its climax in the thirteenth century theologian-philosopher Thomas Aquinas.

Thomas Aquinas, who always spoke of Aristotle as *the* philosopher, as if there were no other, adopted the idea that God can be reached by way of the intellect. He suggested five proofs for the existence of God which were supposed to make God intellectually real to us. To him a person who does not believe in God is essentially a person who cannot follow a logical argument. This view takes us back to Socrates, to whom ignorance and evil seemed the same. There is even a tendency within scholasticism to make a saving virtue out of ignorance. If a man is ignorant, he cannot be held responsible, and thus these theologians assert that people who are pagans or heretics honestly because they don't know any better may be saved by doing that which, though false, is believed by them to be right.

This indicates how much emphasis Christian scholasticism places upon reason and the right use of reason. As Aquinas says, "There are certain things to which even natural reason can attain, for instance that God is, that God is one, and others like these, which even the philosophers proved demonstratively of God, being guided by the light of natural reason." [4]

The rationalistic road to the meaningful life can be found not only in Roman Catholic scholasticism, but also in much that goes as Calvinism or Lutheranism. Wherever the road to God as the source of all value is essentially the road of reason, we deal with rationalism. Wherever Christianity is conceived as a set of logical propositions to which we assent, there reason rules supreme. For example, there are many Lutherans who believe that to be a Lutheran is essentially to hold certain views; to accept certain propositions about Father, Son, and Holy Spirit; or to hold a certain doctrine of the inspiration of Scripture. Especially in what is commonly called "Lutheran Orthodoxy" we confront an approach to God and his truth which is deeply indebted to the Greeks and the medieval scholastics.

In ethics this approach always leads to a withdrawal from the world of conflict. The good and the intel-

[4] Randall, Buchler and Shirk, *Readings in Philosophy* (New York: Barnes & Noble, 1946), p. 263.

lectually correct are identified, and discipleship of the living Christ is reduced to intellectual assent to his wonderful birth, his miracles, and his resurrection. The *good* man is the man who believes right—who knows the right things to believe, understands what is involved and then believes them. Whenever the ultimate meaning of decision is supposed to be an intellectual decision, we deal with rationalism.

We pointed out that the religious search for value can go the way of the will in legalism, the way of the emotions in mysticism and the way of the intellect in rationalism. It may be in order to remind ourselves at this point that these different approaches are in fact never as neatly separated as in this outline. We find both mysticism and rationalism in Jewish religion, legalism in Hinduism. For the sake of classification, however, we can say that these are the basic avenues that man uses to find the source of all value in God. Our own selection is determined by our emotional and intellectual make-up as well as the mood of the age in which we live. But it is undoubtedly true that if we are religious people we are engaged in ascending to God through the discipline of our will, the exercises of our emotions, and/or the cultivation of our intellect. We may even attempt to combine all three.

Though there are many different definitions of religion, in the context of our study religion may be defined as man's search for standards of value. We must emphasize that religion, as we know it through history and see it now, is man's search. Man attempts to find the good life—to approach the Unmoved Mover, as Aristotle called God, or the Architect of the Universe, as the Masons like to call him. It is man who uses whips and mystical incantations, in fastings and frenzied dances, to unite himself with the One, the World Soul, as the mystics see God. It is man who thinks that most rigorous obedience to the divine law forces God, the righteous Judge of the legalists, to declare him fit for the kingdom of heaven. In all the religious search for value God is very real, but the road to God is man's road. It depends on man whether or not he will live the meaningful life. It is man who attempts to save himself. Even in religion, man remains the master of his fate and the captain of his soul. Though the goal is God, it is man who through his efforts makes the achievement of this goal possible.

THE LIFE OF MAN AND THE
JUDGMENT OF GOD

In our discussion so far we have been describing man's efforts to find a basis for making the decisions which life forces upon him. We have recognized that man is committed to decision through the mere fact of his existence, whether he likes it or not. We have joined man in his efforts to figure out how he can possibly make the right decision. We have tried with him to find the basis for right decisions in philosophy and in religion. Thus far we have been concerned solely with the human road to values, the *human* search for God. Now it is time to ask, "How is Christian ethics related to this search? And how does it compare with the answers which man may reach in this religious and philosophical search?"

In answering these questions, another illustration of the human situation may help describe the necessity for decision.

You are a child who is caught in a burning house. Your father is standing under the window, calling to you; but it is dark outside and you cannot see him.

You must either jump or die in the flames. If you jump, your father will catch you. But he can't catch you unless you jump.

Although this illustration breaks down at a number of points, it will serve our purposes. It may be said that after you jump you will realize that you didn't really jump, but were pushed. This, of course, does not help you while the fire is roaring behind you and you feel that the decision is utterly up to you. The theologians will later tell you that you were never as alone as you thought you were, and I am convinced that they are right; but from your point of view, between the empty darkness and the roaring fire, blinded by the fire, you are as alone as a person can be.

In our discussion of man as he deliberates and attempts to make his decisions through philosophy and religion, we have spoken of man *before* he has "jumped" into the arms reaching out to him in the darkness. Christian ethics, on the other hand, is the description of man's situation *after* he has "jumped"—into the arms of God. The Christian life is the life lived in faith in Jesus Christ, the Son of God, the Saviour, who is revealed to us in the Bible and in his holy church. It is significant that we recognize the authority of the Bible and the church only after we "jump."

It is important to remember that we do not cease to be human beings through the jump. Let us now examine the human situation on the basis of our faith in God's invasion into human history, the incarnation of Jesus Christ as promised and proclaimed in the Old

Testament and fulfilled and proclaimed in the New. What is man, with his customs and ideals, with his religious legalism, mysticism and rationalism? What is man who is "bound to be free" in the eyes of God? What is man in the judgment of God?

The Image of God

The biblical answer to this question is simply overwhelming: "Then God said, 'Let us make man in our image, after our likeness.'"[1] In other words, the Bible ascribes to man a uniqueness which distinguishes him profoundly from the rest of creation.

This is a uniqueness which applies to all men. We read in Psalm 139:1-16,

O Lord, thou hast searched me and known me!
Thou knowest when I sit down and when I rise up;
    thou discernest my thoughts from afar.
Thou searchest out my path and my lying down,
    and art acquainted with all my ways.
Even before a word is on my tongue,
    lo, O Lord, thou knowest it altogether.
Thou dost beset me behind and before,
    and layest thy hand upon me.
Such knowledge is too wonderful for me;
    it is high, I cannot attain it.

Whither shall I go from thy Spirit?
    Or whither shall I flee from thy presence?
If I ascend to heaven, thou art there!

[1] Genesis 1:26.

If I make my bed in Sheol, thou art there!
If I take the wings of the morning
    and dwell in the uttermost parts of the sea,
even there thy hand shall lead me
    and thy right hand shall hold me.
If I say, "Let only darkness cover me,
    and the light about me be night,"
even the darkness is not dark to thee,
    the night is bright as the day;
    for darkness is as light with thee.

For thou didst form my inward parts,
    thou didst knit me together in my mother's womb.
I praise thee, for thou art fearful and wonderful.
    Wonderful are thy works!
Thou knowest me right well;
    my frame was not hidden from thee,
when I was being made in secret,
    intricately wrought in the depths of the earth.
Thy eyes beheld my unformed substance;
    in thy book were written, every one of them,
the days that were formed for me,
    when as yet there was none of them.

We have quoted so much of the psalm because it describes the worth of man in relation to God as applying to mankind—not only to the prehistorical creatures of Genesis, but to all men. In the judgment of God, man is unique—for God created him in his image. It is this unique relationship to God which makes man what he is. What the church asserts here is that man is "meaningless" apart from God, that in order to understand man we must understand him in his relationship to God. Every effort to understand man apart from the Creator in whose image he was created is to give up all hope of ever finding the meaning of his life. This is one reason why our efforts so far have seemed fruitless. Philosophically, starting with man, or religiously, starting with man, man cannot be understood. If he is "image," even if he is an utterly distorted image, as we shall see later, he can be understood only in relation to the Original whose image he is.

The special characteristic of man as compared with the rest of creation is that he was created to be *on speaking terms* with God. God speaks to man and man may speak to God. Here the uniqueness of the relationship of God to man is expressed. God did not merely create man through his word as a finished product, but is constantly communicating with him. Or as Emil Brunner puts it, "Figuratively speaking, God produces the other creatures in a finished state; they are what they ought to be, and this they remain. But God retains man within His workshop, within His hands. He does not simply make him and finish him; human nature, indeed, consists in the fact that we may and must remain in the hands of God. The characteristic imprint of man, however, only develops on the basis of the Divine Determination, as an answer to a call, by means of a decision. The necessity for decision, an obligation which he can never evade, is the distinguishing feature of man." [2]

Man is created to be on speaking terms with God. But in order to answer God he must listen. You are not on speaking terms with anybody to whom you are not listening. If your mother-in-law annoys you so much that whenever she speaks to you, you hold your ears shut as an expression of exasperation and defiance, you are not on speaking terms with your mother-in-law. I think it is significant that whenever we are angry with somebody, we won't speak to him. Even little children will say defiantly, "I'll never speak to you, as long as I live"—which generally means half an hour.

Although this ability to hear God and to answer God makes man man, it is not just a natural characteristic like a dog's ability to bark, or a rose's scent; rather it is something which is real only as it is used. And here it again becomes clear how important "decision" is in man's life. A dog is a dog—he cannot decide not to be a dog. A tree is a tree—it cannot decide not to be a tree. But man can decide not to be man; he can refuse to listen to God or talk to him. God spoke to man in love and offered him communion. The time when man thus heard and answered God is a prehistorical time, the *status integritatis*, "the state of integrity" of the theologians. It is not the situation which we find recorded in history. What happened to the relationship between the Creator and the creature created in his image? Man as we discover him in history, man

[2] Brunner, *Man in Revolt* (London: Lutterworth, 1949), p. 97-98.

about whom we read in our newspapers, the man or woman we see when we look into the mirror—they are not the image of God. They are not, properly speaking, "men," if we mean by that the object of God's creative purpose—the being which was to be very good. What happened? Why isn't man what he was created to be? Why isn't man man? The answer to this question lies in the fact that humanity involves decision, and that decision always implies the possibility of wrong decision. The trouble with man is that he made the wrong decision and that he is still making it.

Original Sin and Sins

Man was created to listen to God and to speak to him. Man was created to be loved by God and to love him in return. Man was created to have fellowship with his Creator. But man decided not to listen to God. He decided not to speak to God. Proud of being an image of the Creator, he decided to be the creator. Forgetting that his greatness depended entirely upon his relationship to God, he proudly proceeded to assert his greatness apart from God and thus ceased to be truly man. This development is described in the story of Adam and Eve. There was a first man who could listen to God and speak to God and thus refuse to listen and refuse to speak. Whether you believe that this man lived 6,000 years ago or that he is the product of the evolutionary process is really not too important. What matters is that God created a first being who was different: he could listen, he could speak, he could obey or disobey. And man disobeyed. We know that this disobedience was also partially the result of daemonic powers which encouraged man in his unbelief. The Bible knows of such powers that dwell on man's weakness and encourage him in his revolt against God. Nevertheless, it is of importance for us that the church teaches that man could have followed God—he was not predetermined to disobey; man disobeyed on the basis of his own decision and this disobedience established a pattern which has made it impossible for men ever to obey God out of their own power. The Bible speaks of all men as "by nature children of wrath." [3] The theologians say that original sin means that we inherit not the act of Adam, but rather the revolt against the will of God, a revolt in which we participate from infancy. Original sin is man's revolt against God. Historical man is always "man in revolt." He does not have to learn revolt; he is born in a state of revolt against God. Luther speaks of this sin as "such a deep and evil corruption of nature that no reason understands it, but that it must be believed from the revelation of the Scriptures." It is this sin which is responsible for death; it is the "sickness unto death" of the Bible. Historical man is always the man who is about to die, for sin is as universal as death. Paradise means immortality, history means mortality. According to the Christian faith, we are collectively involved in sin as we are collectively involved in death. We cannot escape the one any more than we can escape the other.

[3] Ephesians 2:3.

If you ask, "Are infants free from sin?" the answer is, "Are infants free from death?" Mankind without exception is involved in sin and death.

We have said that sin is essentially revolt against God. This is a conception of the root of evil quite different from the explanation of the philosophers, to whom evil generally appeared as a deficiency, a lack of something. To Plato evil was "non-being," a minus; an evil man was a man as he existed in the mind of God—minus something which made him less than what he was supposed to be. Evil was a deficiency disease, a pure negation—or, as Socrates put it, ignorance.

In the light of the Scriptures, evil is something far more positive. It is not so much a negation as an assertion, an assertion of man against God. It is man's declaration of independence from God. If we look at the third chapter of Genesis, we find sin described as man's attempt to be equal with God, to assert his freedom from God. In the story of the Tower of Babel men wanted to build a "tower to reach unto heaven."[4] In the New Testament we find this same arrogance and pride at work. In the parable of the Evil Husbandmen,[5] the husbandmen say among themselves after they have killed their master's servants and he has sent his son, "This is the heir; come, let us kill him, and have his inheritance." Again, in the parable of the Prodigal Son the younger son comes to the father saying, "Give me the share of property that falls to me!"[6]

[4] Genesis 11.
[5] Matthew 21:33 f.
[6] Luke 15:11-32.

The story of human sin is the story of man's effort to live without God, to live independently and in revolt against God. Furthermore, since it is man's very nature to live in relationship to God, the story of mankind in history is also the story of man's escape from being man. Man's escape from God is in fact man's escape from himself, for man is truly man only in fellowship with God. This escape from God is at the root of all the evils of human history. When reason, for example, is no longer the human instrument in the service of God it leads to utter irrationality. When freedom is no longer freedom in the service of God, but instead freedom from God, it becomes slavery. It is the cult of reason, the cult of logic of our time which has made the world utterly irrational. The people who claim to be guided by reason alone see in the universe a meaningless and hopeless chaos of electrons and spiral nebulae. The worshipers of independent human reason have made the universe utterly irrational. The worshipers of logic, the logical positivists, have delegated everything that has value to the realm of the meaningless. Similarly, when freedom is merely freedom from God, man becomes utterly unfree. The men who advocate freedom from God have come to the conclusion that man is merely the product of his environment and heredity; that man is what he eats; that he is utterly determined by irrational forces beyond his control; that he is, in the words of C. S. Lewis, merely "a trousered ape." It is the tragedy of sin that it corrupts the very best in man, the very gifts that make man man. It is not merely in his lusts, but particularly in his highest aspirations that sin is most effective. The revolt against God is expressed in our reason, in our morality, in our culture and religion. There is no part of human effort which is not corrupted by sin. The sickness unto death affects all of man.

We have said that the basic sin, psychologically speaking, is pride and self-centeredness. This basic sin of being centered in ourselves rather than in God is at the bottom of all other sins. Every actual sin is an expression of original sin. Every particular sin is an expression of our revolt against God. Man in his effort to organize his life around himself instead of around its true center, God, falls into all sorts of sins. From the point of view of revelation our actual sins are not the occasional moral errors of otherwise well-meaning people; rather they are the result of our basic perversity, our egocentric attempt to organize the universe around ourselves. This attempt starts with the crying infant in his crib, who "unconsciously" attempts to organize the universe, the household into which he is born, around himself (and frequently succeeds in doing so). The effort continues until we die—and even then we attempt through last wills and testaments to keep organizing the universe around our own person, even though this person has passed beyond the point where such organization can give personal satisfaction. Thus my entire life is the proud effort to defy God and to make my own personality the center of everything.

This central position of pride in sin has been very

clearly expressed by C. S. Lewis. He says, "According to Christian teachers, the essential vice, the utmost evil is PRIDE. Unchastity, anger, greed, drunkenness, and all that are mere flea-bites in comparison. It was through Pride that the devil became the devil. Pride leads to every other vice. It is the complete anti-God state of mind." And he continues, "Does this seem to you exaggerated? If so, think it over. I pointed out a moment ago that the more pride one had, the more one disliked pride in others. In fact, if you want to find out how proud you are the easiest way is to ask yourself, 'How much do I dislike it when other people snub me, or refuse to take notice of me or patronize me, or show off?' The point is that each person's pride is in competition with everyone else's pride. It is because I wanted to be the big noise at the party I am so annoyed at someone else being the big noise. Pride is essentially competitive—is competitive by its very nature—while the other vices are competitive only, so to speak, by accident. Pride gets no pleasure out of having something, only out of having more than the next man. We say that people are proud of being rich, or clever, or good looking, but they are not. They are proud of being richer, or cleverer or better looking than others."[7]

Pride enjoys looking down on others. It isn't really money you want, but rather more money than somebody else. Not merely a house, but a bigger or better house than the neighbor's. Not merely a girl, but the

[7] C. S. Lewis, *Christian Behavior* (New York: Macmillan Co., 1943).

other fellow's girl—or vice versa, not merely a fellow, but the other girl's fellow.

Professor Lewis points out that some vices bring people together—drunkenness, unchastity, or gluttony can create some sort of fellowship—but pride always divides people, separates them from each other and makes them into enemies.

What is worse, pride separates us hopelessly from God. Because it is the very nature of God to be above us, and pride cannot tolerate anything above it, pride therefore separates us effectively from God. This is as true of religious pride as it is of irreligious pride. Irreligious people are often separated from God by the animal vices, such as greed and unchastity, but religious people are separated from God through pride. It is the religious sin, the sin of the Pharisees and all their numerous descendants, and it is the sin which most effectively cuts us off from God. Our Lord could work with prostitutes and thieving tax collectors, for they were sinners who knew that they sinned. The Pharisees, on the other hand, had lost all perspective because of their pride. Pride is the sin that is camouflaged as virtue, the sin that can drive out other sins and yet keep us effectively and indefinitely from God. Pride keeps some people from all sorts of evils, from adultery, from theft, from dishonesty. They are too proud to lie or to steal even other people's wives. But this same pride also keeps them from God. They are too proud to look up to God, to know themselves as sinners that need his forgiveness and children that need his fatherly love.

Defiantly, they insist that man stands alone, that he is the "weary but unyielding Atlas," in the words of Russell,[8] upon whom all hope, all decency, all goodness rest. It is pride that keeps us from jumping into the outstretched arms of God.

Pride as revolt against God is the basic sin of man. All our many sins—catalogues of which can be found in the New Testament—are expressions of this revolt. They are effects of the basic revolt and at the same time our way of continuing in our state of revolt against God. Man looked at from the point of view of the revelation of God in Jesus Christ is always a sinner. In everything he does he asserts himself against God and revolts against the Creator. There are actions that are better than others from the point of view of law—even divine law. But even an action that is better is not necessarily good. After we have done all things we are still unprofitable servants. Man has always been a sinner and will always be a sinner. Sin has effectively cut man off from the fellowship with God for which he was created. Sin has effectively destroyed the image of God in man, leaving a mere remnant. Man has not become an animal. He is still man, but in a hopeless situation. Created to receive his meaning from fellowship with God—from being on speaking terms with God—he now exists in revolt against God. Neither real man nor animal, he is a being whose meaning is meaninglessness, whose hope is hopelessness. He is a being who knows what love is but lives hate, who knows what

[8] Bertrand Russell, *Selected Papers,* p. 15.

peace is but lives in restlessness and war, who knows what life is and yet whose living is dying. Knowing of heaven, he is bound for hell. This is the situation of man as the result of sin. This is the judgment of God on man's pride and revolt.

We have looked at man's predicament under the judgment of God psychologically and found that it was pride; if we now look at it theologically we find that it is unbelief. Man's predicament is that he who was created by the love of God to trust in God lives in unbelief and distrust. Pride in relationship to God is unbelief: we do not even believe that he is God. We live as if there were no God. And yet somehow we know that we are not really alone, that we are not merely whistling in the dark. Somehow we know that we are not really the Atlas that carries the universe. Somehow we know that we are not the masters of our fate or the captains of our soul. God is all about us. In him we live and move and have our being—and yet we do not believe. Theologically speaking, unbelief is the basic sin, the ultimate sin: unbelief in the love of God in the very face of this love; unbelief in death in the very face of death; and unbelief in the judgment of God in the very face of this judgment.

Man looked at from the point of view of revelation looks far different from the man we discussed philosophically and religiously so far. In the light of revelation, man is incurably ill. His disease is sin, the "sickness unto death." It is a disease which he has contracted voluntarily but which he cannot get rid of voluntarily. It is a disease that affects and corrupts everything he does but above all a disease that sepa1ates him from his Creator and condemns him to meaninglessness and hopelessness. The disease creates many outward signs. We could mention the traditional capital vices as examples—pride, envy, anger, covetousness, sloth, gluttony, and lust. But theologically speaking, we must say all these characteristics of the disease are expressions of one basic trouble—the chief sin from which all others descend is unbelief. It is because man does not believe in God that he cannot live a meaningful life. As long as unbelief rules men's hearts the Christian life is impossible. It is unbelief which separates man from God, unbelief which brings him into the judgment, unbelief that dooms him for all eternity. Man created in God's image becomes through unbelief a caricature. Created to reveal God's love, he chooses to reveal God's wrath and judgment. But lest we blame all this on a prehistorical ancestor we must keep in mind that before God our own unbelief is as real as the unbelief of Adam and Eve. We are all in this together. We share in the guilt of Adam and Eve and they share in ours. As Kierkegaard put it, "The man whom God c1eated is always both this individual and humanity." Because man sins he is a sinner, and because he is a sinner he sins, said Emil Brunner. Even though we may never fully understand this fact, the result of it is clearly before our eyes. The wages of sin is death. And we all die.

THE LIFE OF MAN AND THE
LAW OF GOD

Man is created in the image of God. Man is created on speaking terms with God, but man revolts against his Creator, refusing to listen to him, speak to him, or believe in him. The result of this revolt is utter catastrophe. Hate, jealousy, greed, lust, sickness, despair, and finally death, are all results of man's unbelief, of man's basic sin. But somehow, despite our unbelief, despite man's revolt against God, the world keeps going. If man were left to his own devices of unbelief, we would expect a greater chaos than in fact exists. The reason for the relative order which prevents man from completely destroying himself and his fellow-men is found in the divine law.

God has established a moral law which keeps the world in a semblance of order in spite of sin and its catastrophic results. Left to his own selfishness and pride, man would indeed be in the position which Thomas Hobbes, the great British philosopher, believed to be the original state of man—namely, a war of all against all. This would be a merciless attempt of individual men to organize the world around themselves, an attempt which would make all order impossible and bring utter ruin and destruction to man's universe.

That this is not in fact the case, that we have a semblance of order in our families, in our social life, in our political and economic life, is the result of divine natural law. This is not a "law of nature" independent of God. For nature is never independent of God. In every moment it is maintained by God's almighty creating and preserving power. But this divine natural law is one of God's means of dealing with his creation. The God who created men and who has a purpose for them in spite of their unbelief and disobedience has established "orders of preservation" which keep men from following completely their revolutionary tendencies and destroying their world and themselves.

The reason for the divine natural law is that God wants to give men an opportunity to be confronted by the Gospel. It is a device of his patience, giving men time to repent and change. A wealthy father who has an utterly irresponsible son may make a will which will make it impossible for the son to waste his inheritance and destroy himself completely. The son will think of his father's will as a cruel and mean restriction of his freedom. But perhaps the will allows the son time to grow up. Perhaps he does come into full possession of his inheritance by the time he reaches the age of thirty-five or forty or fifty. So God has given us his divine natural law which restrains our sinful human irresponsibility for a time. Perhaps God, too, will leave us to our own devices when the time has come to bring human history to its climactic end, and perhaps this time is nearer than we think.

Be that as it may, God has instituted his divine natural law. What is it like?

The Nature of Divine Law

God's natural law is part of the structure of the universe. It is not something we have to discover in order to make it real, for it exists quite apart from our awareness or unawareness of it.

When we think of natural law, we generally think of something like the law of gravity. And in a sense the law of gravity is a good illustration of God's law even as it operates in the realm of human decision—in human life. The significant thing about the law of gravity is that it is not really a law, but a description of the way in which things operate. They operate this way whether you know the law or not. If you know it, you can keep it in mind in your actions and avoid a good deal of difficulty, and even if you don't know it as a "law," you know the facts that it describes. If we ever had ancestors who jumped from tree to tree—and I have my doubts about it—they certainly knew nothing about a "law of gravity." But as they jumped from tree to tree, they realized that if they'd miss the next branch they'd fall flat on their faces. Quite without any knowledge of the theory behind it, the facts of the matter were abundantly clear to them. In other words, the law of gravity and all other so-called "laws" of the natural sciences are merely convenient basic descriptions of natural phenomena which scientists have observed to be invariable. Because these phenomena are invariable they are named "laws."

Now, the divine natural law operates in a very similar manner. It is not, strictly speaking, a legal code which was written down and whose force and power depends on its public proclamation. On the contrary, the power of the divine natural law resides in the fact that it describes accurately how things are.

You don't have to be a philosopher or a theologian to discover certain basic moral laws at work in the universe. For example, let us assume for the moment that there is no religious or social injunction against lying, that lying is neither right nor wrong. It is my claim that the person who would constantly and consistently lie, who would always tell a falsehood with the intent to deceive rather than the truth, would become effectively dumb. He would no longer be understood by other human beings, for the fact of the matter is simply that language is based upon a minimum amount of honesty. If you say "chair" you must mean chair. If you say "chair" and mean "table" and say "table" and mean "ceiling," say "brown" and mean "hot," you are simply no longer understandable to anybody else. If you say "The brown chair is in the kitchen" and mean "The Buick is in the garage" you are not communicating effectively. And after you have done this for a little while, nobody will listen to you, for you will have lost your ability to speak.

Speech is not merely sound, but rather sound which communicates meaning; and in order to communicate effectively, a certain amount of honesty is essential. Quite apart from any religion or social law, lying makes any man effectively dumb. In fact, even in order to be an effective liar you must be an honest person; if you always lie, people won't believe you even when you are telling the truth. This is simply one of the basic moral laws that you may ignore only if you are willing to take the consequences.

There are other examples of divine natural law in operation. Plato pointed out in his *Republic* that even a band of robbers is only as effective as the remnant of honor that exists among the thieves. People that are utterly dishonest make poor robbers. The lookout has to look out and not just stand around. However evil his job is, he has to do it well and be trustworthy about it if the thieves are to be successful. We find another example in the relationship of the sexes. It is simply not true that all sexual behavior is equally good. After the Russian Revolution in 1917 when the Soviet government attempted to abolish the laws protecting the family, the results were so disastrous that they soon changed the laws again and now protect marriage more carefully than most states in America. The protection of the family is essential for the preservation of society, and whenever men undermine it, the results are immediately disastrous. If we should pass a law making homosexuality socially acceptable and legally right, it would not for a moment change the fact that homosexuality if generally practiced destroys civilization, as was demonstrated by the Greeks and Romans. In the first chapter of St. Paul's Epistle to the Romans, we find a reference to this established fact of divine natural law. He says, "For the wrath of God is revealed from heaven against all ungodliness and wickedness of men who by their wickedness suppress the truth. For what can be known about God is plain to them, because God has shown it to them." [1]

These laws are not inventions of men. They simply exist as a part of the structure of the world in which we live—and if we attempt to break them, they break us. It isn't very important whether or not you and I believe there is a law of gravity so long as we keep in mind that it exists. The law of gravity is real whether we like it or not; it is equally real for the physics professor who knows all about it, and for the baby who leans too far out of his crib. With or without our approval, it simply is. Similarly, the divine natural law simply exists, quite apart from our knowledge or approval, and anybody who consistently breaks it discovers that it eventually breaks him.

While it is fairly easy to see that some such basic law exists, it is far more difficult to describe the specific content. In fact, all efforts to set down in detail the specific rules which constitute divine natural law prove misleading and futile. The reason for this state of affairs is that sin has made it impossible for us to see clearly even the divine natural law. We said before

[1] Romans 1:18, 19.

that sin affects every aspect of our life and personality. It also affects our understanding of God's natural law. Though this law exists and is effective, man perceives it only haphazardly and within the confusion of his sin-perverted nature.

But man does know something about this law. The Apostle Paul says, "Ever since the creation of the world his [God's] invisible nature, namely, his eternal power and deity, has been clearly perceived in the things that have been made." [2] This natural knowledge of God's law is indicated in the moral codes of all nations and peoples. It is true that a comparative study of the moral codes of various nations reveals many striking differences. Yet it is a fact, far more amazing and little mentioned in our day, that wherever you go there are certain basic human relationships which are ruled by law. There is a great deal of moral confusion, but the basic laws everywhere deal with the same problems and serve to restrain man. Among all peoples laws order the relationship of parents and children—the responsibility of the generations toward each other. Everywhere law orders the relationships of life and limits man in his desire to take the lives of those he does not like. Of course, there is a tremendous difference between Pennsylvania Quakers and New Guinea headhunters—but the difference is rather in the scope of the prohibition than in the prohibition. Even the headhunters have laws that prevent them from taking the lives of their fellows in the same tribe

[2] Romans 1:20.

or village. Everywhere there are laws about the sex relationship. There are tremendous variations, and anybody interested in the subject may read Ford and Beach's somewhat superficial but nevertheless valuable study, *Patterns of Sexual Behaviour*.[3] But the amazing thing is that the patterns exist; everywhere among human beings, the sex urge is restrained. And in so-called primitive societies the sanctions against the offender are in general more strict than in the so-called advanced societies. Nowhere is sexual behavior a matter of indifference to society; everywhere there is law. Similarly, truth and property are protected by laws everywhere. In spite of all variations, a common pattern can be observed.

Law exists, and the laws of mankind are attempts, more or less adequate, to codify the law of God which confronts man in the very structure of the world.

Now the question arises, what is the purpose of this law for human life? Why has God given a law to men who in their state of sinful revolution will to break it anyway? Furthermore, because of sin, mankind cannot even clearly comprehend the nature of this divine natural law and is therefore bound to fail when confronted by it. What good does the law do? What is its use?

The answer to this question is twofold. The divine natural law has two uses, a theological use and a political use.

[3] New York: Harpers, 1951.

The Proper Use of the Law

From the point of view of Christianity, the basic use, the theological use, the proper use of the law is that it shows man in the judgment of God. It accuses man before the face of God. Melanchthon says, in the Apology to the Augsburg Confession, "*Lex semper accusat*," or, "The law always accuses." God uses the law to show us that we are sinners, and we can use the law in order that we might see our hopeless situation before the throne of God. Whereas the legalist believes that the law is a means by which man can justify himself before God, that it is a means to force God to accept us into his kingdom, the New Testament sees in the law a means to reveal man's situation in the judgment of God—to show man in revolt. The primary task of the law is entirely negative.

In his Letter to the Romans, Paul says that man can know God, but because of his sin he knows him only as judge. And the law always accuses us before this judge. Paul writes about the Gentiles, "So they are without excuse; for although they knew God they did not honor him as God or give thanks to him, but they became futile in their thinking and their senseless minds were darkened." Later he continues, "And since they did not see fit to acknowledge God, God gave them up to a base mind and to improper conduct. They were filled with all manner of wickedness, evil, covetousness, malice. Full of envy, murder, strife, deceit, malignity, they are gossips, slanderers, haters of God, insolent, haughty, boastful, inventors of evil, disobedient to parents, foolish, faithless, heartless, ruthless. Though they know God's decree that those who do such things deserve to die, they not only do them but approve those who practice them."[4] St. Paul continues, "Therefore you have no excuse, O man, whoever you are . . ." The law always accuses.

Paul writes in I Timothy 1:9, ". . . The law is not laid down for the just but for the lawless and disobedient, for the ungodly and sinners . . ." The law always accuses!

From the point of view of the Christian the main function of the divine law is that it shows man the hopelessness of his situation. It is like the fever thermometer: it cures no ill, but helps sick people to realize they are sick and in need of a doctor. If properly used, the law shows us the hopelessness of our predicament and makes us ready to accept the Gospel of the Lord Jesus Christ.

The Political Use of the Law

The law has another, even if secondary, function. We indicated it in our introduction to this chapter. The law, though always accusing, though never obeyed, helps to keep this world in a semblance of order until history has reached its end, until God intervenes in his last judgment.

Through the divine natural law, God has established certain orders like marriage and the family and the social, economic, and political order which are designed

[4] Romans 1:28-32.

to make life possible in spite of the self-destructive power of sin. The protection of these orders constitutes the "political use" of the law. Under God's law society has a responsibility to protect the family, to protect life, to protect property from wanton destruction, to protect men against each other and against themselves.

It is important for us to remember that God has not established one particular form of social organization but has given basic rules for all social organization. The Golden Rule is a concise summary of the principles that must govern all social institutions if they are to protect society against self-destruction. It is significant that such laws appear not only on Christian soil but also among the pagans. Far from detracting from the absolute value of Christianity they further substantiate what the New Testament has said about the law as being written into the hearts of all men. Roman Stoics and Chinese Confucians, people everywhere agree amazingly about some basic rules for all men.

But even the "political use" of the law, which helps to preserve order and confine somewhat the anarchic character of sin, always shows man as sinner. We ought to know that men are equal, that they have certain inalienable rights, that among these rights are life, liberty, and the pursuit of happiness. We may say that we do know, but even the nation which has incorporated this insight into one of her basic political documents constantly and publicly offends against this very principle. To give just one example, Christian citizens of a large city in a northern state refused burial in their cemetery to a man killed in one of our wars fighting for these same fine Christian citizens. The reason: the dead soldier was an Indian!

In our discussion of the nature and the use of God's natural law we have come to the conclusion that the law exists as part of the structure of the world in which we live. It exists quite apart from our recognition or our obedience to it. It is at the root of all the practical efforts to codify and write down laws. Yet none of these efforts is fully successful. They are merely more or less adequate attempts to describe the way in which the world in fact operates. Divine natural law is part of this world as it confronts us.

The purpose of the law is twofold. Its theological purpose, its basic purpose from our point of view, is its accusing function. The law accuses man, revealing him to himself and before God as a lawbreaker, as a man in revolt.

The second function of the law is to supply the basis for a fairly well-ordered organization of society, to establish marriage and family, government and society. In its second function, the law is also hindered by human sin, but it does establish a somewhat workable pattern which keeps mankind from utter anarchy and chaos. But even in this political function, the law remains the eternal accuser of sinful man. The law never justifies man. It always accuses him.

Modern Man and the Law of God

While the divine law has been a very real force in the life of men in all times, modern man has thought he could ignore this law. The relativism and naturalism we have previously discussed are efforts to act as if there were no law and man could really do as he pleases. We have had people at all times who defied the divine law, who did what they knew to be wrong and somehow hoped to get away with it. But in our time we have a large number of people everywhere who simply deny that there is such a thing as right and wrong. Some of them claim that man is merely an animal and that nothing an animal does is ever right or 'wrong. It simply is. An action may not be useful for man's survival but it is never "wrong." In this manner they attempt to free man from the accusing finger of the law. Others again claim that every man is the product of circumstances over which he has no control. He is determined by what is commonly called "environment" or "heredity." Nothing he does is right or wrong, because he has no choice about it anyway. Every man does what he has to do. Here, too, it is claimed that the law does not accuse us any longer.

Many modern men think they have effectively escaped the divine natural law as it stands accusingly before us. But what is the result? First of all, the law still exists; no effort on our part can wipe it out. You may, if you wish, design a very clever theory that there is really no law of gravity, but if you lean too far out of a second-floor window of your home, you'll fall down

—even though according to your theory it shouldn't happen. The universe is not run according to your theories about gravity. Similarly we may all take a vote, we may move, second, and pass unanimously that there is no moral law in the universe—but that does not for a moment change the facts. The universe does not run by our theories about morality either. This fact becomes clear in the literature of our age. Much of our literature is said to be "realistic," meaning that it attempts to describe things as they really are. As a result, it describes modern man as being broken by the world in which he has to live. Victorian-age novelists and dramatists often attempted to point a moral, and often failed because they tried too hard. Our writers are trying to describe things as they "really" are. They do not believe in a divine natural law that governs the universe, but, as they describe people as they "really" are, they show only too plainly that man (we know him to be a sinful man) is broken by the world in which he lives (we know it as the world governed by God's law.)

Our secular authors would say, "Man always loses; he can't win; the cards are stacked against him; the dice are loaded." This is merely observing the surface. We know on the basis of the revelation in Jesus Christ that the wages of sin is death. The law always accuses—whether you like it or not, whether you believe in it or not. In a sense, Eugene O'Neill or Tennessee Williams or *Death of a Salesman* are better reading for us than some of the sentimental and silly self-improvement books by preachers and would-be preachers who tell us that all we have to do is to keep a stiff upper lip—or keep smiling or take our breathing exercises— and everything will be fine and life will be beautiful as "peace of mind" and "peace of soul" immediately descend upon us. Try substituting Norman Mailer for Dale Carnegie. The world is just as tough as our most realistic writers can describe it. The reason, however, is hidden from them. We know the reason—the law accuses all of us always, the wages of sin is death.

Furthermore, the result of all this is anxiety and despair. Modern man may not fear God as his ancestors did once upon a time, but he is more afraid than they ever were. To the people that feared God the universe seemed orderly and meaningful. To modern man the universe is utterly meaningless. Modern man is haunted not by the fear of God or the fear of the devil, but by the fear of nothing. This fear of nothing is a very serious form of mental illness which cannot be easily overcome. If you fear God, you might be able to find peace with God. If you fear nothing, you can't find peace with nothing. As a result, our situation as men and women of the twentieth century is, if anything, a little worse than the human situation has been for some time. We have attempted to escape from God but this is harder than to escape from ourselves. "Whither shall I go from thy Spirit? Or whither shall I flee from thy presence? If I ascend to heaven, thou art there! If I make my bed in Sheol thou art there! If I take the wings of the morning and dwell in the uttermost parts of the sea, even there thy hand shall lead me, and thy right hand shall hold me." [5]

It is impossible to escape from God. It is impossible to escape from his law. All human efforts to do so end in despair. It is man's peculiar position to know God and yet ever to attempt to escape from him, to know his law and yet always to be accused by it. Historical man lives in an eternal contradiction. Created for fellowship with God, he attempts vainly to be an animal. Pascal says, "What a chimera then is man! What a novelty! What a monster, what a chaos, what a contradiction, what a prodigy! . . . Judge of all things, imbecile worm of the earth; depository of the truth, a sink of uncertainty and error; the pride and refuse of the Universe." [6] This is a picture of man, the most dreadful picture of failure. Yet this is not the end of the story. The life of man under the Gospel begins only when man has broken down completely as the result of sin and law.

[5] Psalm 139:7-10.
[6] Pascal, *Pensees*, Fragment 434.

PART II

THE LIFE OF MAN UNDER THE GOSPEL

THE NATURE OF THE GOSPEL

To man caught in the web of sin, to man doomed to failure and death, to man lost, comes the Gospel of Jesus Christ. The word "gospel" means literally "good news." Now, what is the good news the Gospel brings?

Man's situation is not hopeless. Man does not stand alone. Death is not the end. What we see in nature—that might makes right, that the big animal eats the little—is not the true pattern.

The true pattern of the universe has been revealed in the Jesus Christ who was born of the Virgin Mary in a dilapidated shack in a dilapidated country, who lived and worked and was executed under Pontius Pilate and on the third day rose from the dead, defeating death not only for his own person, but for all mankind. He is the second Adam. Just as in Adam all men sinned—not in the sense that they were not responsible, but in the sense that the pattern was established in which they would follow—so in Jesus Christ *all men are saved*. Not in the sense that they can do nothing about it, for they are not automatically saved; but in the sense that an alternative pattern has been established. We who have said "Yes" to Adam and to sin may also say "Yes" to Christ and salvation. Just as our acceptance of Adam established a pattern of doom and death, so our "Yes" to Christ establishes a pattern of hope and salvation. "God was in Christ reconciling the world to himself." [1] "For God so loved the world, that he gave his only Son, that whoever believes in him should not perish, but have eternal life." [2]

This is the Gospel. I realize that it sounds old and time-worn. But that is merely because we all have heard it too often without listening. It is still the greatest news in the world, the only news that really counts. It is the only basis for a meaningful life, for a Christian life.

It would be the task of a study of the Christian faith to analyze in detail what this Gospel means. And then we would still only deal with the surface facts. Nobody—ever—can exhaust the full meaning. In our study of the Christian life we must stress that the "Yes" to this Gospel is the *beginning of the Christian life*. It is the leap of faith about which we have spoken many times before. Without this leap, without this faith, the Christian life is not possible. The Christian life begins with faith—and all the activities, all the "good works" of the Christian must be a result of this faith, or they are not good. "The first and highest, the most precious of all good works is faith in

[1] II Corinthians 5:19.
[2] John 3:16.

Christ."[3] "Faith alone makes all other works good, acceptable, and worthy."[4]

Faith is belief in Christ. It is significant that no other word of the vocabulary of the evangelical Christian church has suffered such sad transformations as this word "believe." We have made the most profound expression of Christianity into a word that in everyday life expresses uncertainty and doubt. The reason is that the words "I believe" mean something entirely different when applied to things than when applied to persons. When you say "I believe it is going to rain tomorrow," you are saying in fact, "I don't know for sure," or, "Perhaps it is going to rain." The same is true about all other objects. If I say I believe that Harrisburg is the capital of Pennsylvania, I again express doubt; I don't know for sure. This means clearly that whenever the words "I believe" are used in connection with objects they express not what Christians call *faith*, but what we call *doubt*.

The situation changes as soon as we use these same words in connection with a person. Let us say that your best friend has been accused of stealing. You are confronted by this report—and then you answer, "I believe in John." You are not saying "I don't know, perhaps he did steal." You are not even saying he didn't steal whatever has been stolen. But you are making the supreme assertion that you can possibly make in regard to another person. When you say "I

[3] Luther, *A Treatise on Good Works*, Phila. Edition, Vol. I, p. 187.
[4] Ibid., p. 190.

believe in John" you are saying "John is incapable of stealing—he is incapable of doing anything mean and shoddy!" You are here expressing your faith. When we talk about the Christian faith which is at the beginning of the Christian life, and without which this life cannot be lived, we are talking about faith in *Christ, the Son of God, the Saviour.*

If we say "We believe in Jesus Christ as our personal Saviour," we are saying a lot more than that we believe that he was born in a miraculous manner, or that he was able to perform miracles, or that he was a good man, or that he died innocently, or even that he rose from the dead. All these things are facts about his life, which we may or may not believe. I think that the devil himself believes these facts. But he merely believes facts about Christ; he does not believe in Christ. The Christian life begins with this faith in a person, with this act of confidence. It is *this* faith that makes all works *good*—and where this faith is lacking, they are *evil*.

Luther explained the relationship between this faith and the works of the Christian life by using the illustration of a young couple that are truly in love. When you are in love with a person, you do not evaluate his or her acts and deeds according to any other standard than the standard of your love. That's why a flower, a corsage may become so very important. It isn't really the flower, but the love which is expressed in and with this flower. People in love sometimes save the stubs of the tickets of a show that they have attended together, not because these stubs have any intrinsic value—for in fact they are absolutely worthless—but they are again expressions and reminders of that which transforms all other facts: their love.

The relationship between people in love is not based upon any other outside standard. They do not measure the deeds they do for each other, the presents they give each other, the letters they write each other, by the standards that are generally used. If the person you love drives six hundred miles to see you, you don't appreciate this at the rate of six cents a mile. To you it is an expression of love, and measured in terms of this love. In the same manner, you do not evaluate the cufflinks or the bracelet given you by the one you love in terms of their current value at the nearest pawn shop. If people act this way, they certainly are not in love. When you get a letter from the person you love, you don't judge it as English literature; you don't count the split infinitives and the spelling errors, for the letter, too, is an expression of the reality of love.

So must it be also in the Christian life wherein the person-to-person relationship of faith is the basic fact. What men call good works must be measured entirely in relation to this fact of faith. Only in faith are our works "good," and without this faith no work is good. Faith is this complete trust, this complete confidence in God and his love toward you. It is this daily jumping into the outstretched arms of the God you cannot see but who you know will always be there to catch you.

THE NATURE OF CHRISTIAN FAITH

Now we want to look at the Christian life from the point of view of this faith. And in order that we might see all the various aspects of life in the light of faith we shall follow the division of life as we find it in the Ten Commandments. These commandments deal with the various areas of life which God can transform for us through his grace. In this "leaping" faith we lay hold on this grace of God. Through faith these commandments are changed from the accusing law to a description of the possibilities of the Christian life. They are no longer the terrifying study of what we must do for God, and cannot do, but rather, when looked at from the point of view of the Gospel, they become a description of what God can make out of our life if we let him.

This is what Luther does in his *Treatise on Good Works*. He takes the Ten Commandments and looks at them through the Gospel and they become the description of the glorious possibilities of the life of the children of God. In our description of the Christian life we want to follow Luther's method, look at the

Ten Commandments and see what God can do with all the various parts of our life if we lay hold of his grace in faith.

The First Commandment: "I am the Lord thy God. Thou shalt have no other gods before Me."

According to Luther, faith is the work of the first commandment, which says, "Since I alone am God, thou shalt place all thy confidence, trust, and faith on me alone and on no one else."[1] Of course, for Christians this is no longer a commandment in the sense of the law as we studied it before. Rather it is an expression of faith, a kind of confidence and trust which we can have only as a gift from God. Thus, in order to be able to fulfill this first commandment of the Christian life upon which all others depend, it is necessary that God through his grace must have made this trust possible. Ultimately, faith is always a miracle. Once we recognize the desperate situation in which man finds himself as the result of sin, we know that out of our own power we cannot fulfill the first or any other commandment. It is God who through his grace makes the fulfillment of any of the commandments possible.

But what is the relation of our faith to the grace of God? What can we do to contribute to our salvation? Here Christian ethics says an eternal "no" to all the efforts to make ethics some means of becoming well-pleasing to God. It is impossible to do any good work outside of faith. "All works without faith are idolatry."

[1] *A Treatise on Good Works,* p. 194.

says Luther.[2] They are "splendid vices," as St. Augustine puts it. Remember, it is not the intrinsic value of the work that is significant, but only that it must be an expression of faith.

And this faith is the gift of the *divine grace*. In this relationship, man is like a drowning person who cannot swim but who thinks he can swim. As he is coming up for the last time a good swimmer sees him from the shore. He jumps in, swims to him, and pulls him out, saving his life. Thus it is with divine grace. Man cannot save himself; in fact, if he insists to the lifeguard on doing it his own way, he will drown. The best thing he can do is to hold still and let the lifeguard do the saving. Many a man has drowned because he wanted to be saved on his own terms, to bargain with the lifeguard, to suggest his own superb lifesaving technique which he read somewhere.

Perhaps another illustration of divine grace will be helpful. A man sits in a dark room with all the shades drawn. He does not want any bright sunlight in the room, but there is one shade which will not catch; in order to keep it down he has to hold it down with his own hands. Suddenly he can hold it no longer, the shade rolls up and sunlight floods the room. You and I are this man and God works on us through the mechanism of the spring and the sun that shines on the outside—if you don't mind the comparison—through the law and through the Gospel. Finally we let go, not because we want to, but because God has overcome

[2] Ibid., p. 195.

our revolt. Some people hold out longer than others. Some people hold out forever—and that is hell. But nobody lets go because of his own goodness and love. It is the goodness and love of God, the grace of God, that raises the shade so that we may have faith.

When through the grace of God faith is in our hearts, all works that we do become good works. They are good because they are an expression of our trust in God, and only insofar as they express this trust.

Luther says faith is like health and the good works are like the use of our limbs that health makes possible. When we speak of the all-importance of faith, we do not say that works are not good, but we say that faith is necessary to make good works possible. "Therefore when some say that good works are forbidden when we preach faith alone, it is as if I said to a sick man 'If you had health, you would have the use of all your limbs; but without health, the works of all your limbs are nothing' and he wanted to infer that I had forbidden the works of all his limbs; whereas on the contrary, I meant that he must first have health, which will work all the works of all the members. So faith also must be in all works the master workman and captain, or they are nothing at all." [3]

This description of faith as perfect trust in God seems to be in striking contrast to our daily life and our daily temptations. But it is faith to believe that God can save us in spite of ourselves, that he is willing to forgive our sins—not because we deserve it, but because he is love.

[3] A Treatise on Good Works, p. 199.

CHRISTIAN DISCIPLESHIP

The Second Commandment: "Thou shalt not take the Name of the Lord thy God in vain: for the Lord will not hold him guiltless that taketh His Name in vain."

For the life under the Gospel the first commandment deals with the importance of faith for the Christian life. The second commandment deals with the praise of God and the confession of his name which this faith makes necessary. The praise of God is the main result of faith.

And this is the life in the presence of God, or the life of discipleship, that whatever we do and wherever we do it, we do it in the presence of God and as disciples of Jesus Christ. It is not necessary to be spectacular in our discipleship, to run around in odd costumes or take a vow never to speak again. It is important that wherever we are we should praise God. The less attention our life draws to ourselves and the more attention it draws to our Lord and Master, the more surely it is lived in obedience to the second commandment. It is at this point that pride enters the Christian life most easily—pride, the most spiritual of all sins because it is not even recognized as a sin.

It is in suffering and dishonor that we have the greatest opportunity to give praise to God. When things are difficult, in times of sorrow and suffering, we have the greatest opportunity to praise God by being disciples of Christ.

It isn't much of a trick to live a superficially happy life according to the suggestions of Aristotle. He says that in order to be happy one ought to be free—that is, not to have to do any menial work, and to have good health, an independent and substantial income, a beautiful wife, attractive and healthy children. Aristotle says that unless one has these "raw materials" in a reasonable degree, it is impossible to be happy.

It is here that Christianity is utterly different from all that paganism ever had to offer. Even hardship and suffering are for Christians opportunities to come closer to God, not only in theory, but also in practice. There seems to be an inverse ratio between our prosperity and our willingness to praise God and call upon him. This is true of individuals, and it is no less true of entire nations. When we read the New Testament, we are astonished that so few of the well-to-do members of society were willing to follow Christ. But he explained it: "It is easier for a camel to go through the eye of a needle, than for a rich man to enter into the kingdom of God." [1] Neither the rich, nor members of the master-race (in Jesus' time the Jews were the advocates of the

[1] Matthew 19:24.

master-race theory) have an easy time. On the other hand, the Samaritans, the racial outcasts who were the victims of the Jewish version of "Jim Crowism," were eager to follow Christ, as were the women. In all those societies where women have been little better off than animals, where they have been suffering under unjust laws, they have been willing to be disciples.

Individually, it is through suffering that you and I grow in grace. Kierkegaard tells the story of a man riding in a stagecoach through an evening landscape, with a lantern burning brightly next to him on the seat. Suddenly a gust of wind blows out the light; all becomes dark about him, and for the first time on his journey, he can look up into the sky and see the stars. It is often through suffering—physical, but above all spiritual suffering—that men are made aware of their relationship to God.

It is therefore dangerous to speak of suffering as something that Christianity can prevent or take away. It is not true that Christians do not suffer pain, that they do not suffer spiritual torments, that they are always "well-adjusted," or that they always keep smiling and cannot be perturbed by anything that might possibly occur. On the contrary, the cost of discipleship is often very high. Not only do the life and death of Jesus Christ indicate this, but also the lives of all great Christians, from the apostles to Dietrich Bonhoeffer who wrote *The Cost of Discipleship* and was murdered by his Nazi jailers in the concentration camp at Flossenburg. It is often through suffering that men become aware of the precariousness of their situation, of their predicament as men. For this reason Luther can say, "For this is the most dangerous trial of all, when there is no trial and everything is and goes well; for then a man is tempted to forget God, to become too bold and to misuse the times of prosperity." [2]

Luther points out that peace and tranquility often bring out the worst in man. This was certainly true of the Hebrews of old, and its truth seems to be illustrated in modern America as well, in such periods as the "Roaring Twenties." If there is something like a return to religion in our day, as contrasted with the Roaring Twenties of our parents, a return which affects even youth, then the reason must be that we are more aware than our parents of the precariousness of human existence. We no longer believe, as they did, that history is "redemptive," that all we have to do is to sit tight and things will work out, that progress is assured, and that "tomorrow will be better." On the contrary, most of us fear that tomorrow might be worse.

However, we have learned again through the suffering and disappointments of our age that all adversity and suffering can become God's means to push us over the brink and into his arms. Through suffering we are often forced into a clear-cut decision in our relationship to God.

In his *Treatise on Good Works* Luther mentions other works of the second commandment but to him the most important of all its meanings is preaching. The second commandment obligates the Christian to protect and proclaim God's holy name against all his enemies.

It is here that the revolutionary character of Christianity becomes especially obvious. Luther says, "here we must stir up against us the *rich, learned, holy,* and all that is of repute in the world . . . every Christian is obliged to do so!" [3]

Out of faith in the Gospel we must resist all wrong. And this means particularly to fight against the wrong done to the poor, the despised, and our enemies.[4] It is very simple to fight against the wrong that is done by those who have no power, who cannot defend themselves, who cannot make any trouble. Anybody can do this and almost everybody does it. It is much more difficult to fight the wrongs done by the powerful, the rich, and our friends.

For illustration, we might look at certain interesting sociological facts. We know that the rate of juvenile delinquency is far higher in poorer neighborhoods than in rich neighborhoods. This disparity cannot simply be written off to the established fact that poverty breeds crime. Often another factor enters the picture, the difference between law enforcement practices in the suburbs and in the slums. If a youngster breaks a window in the wealthy neighborhood, and his father is well-to-do, he won't be arrested. He may possibly be reprimanded, but in any case daddy pays for a new

---

[3] A Treatise on Good Works, p. 217.
[4] Ibid.

window and the case is closed. But the youngster in the slums whose father is a drunkard will go before juvenile court. It is much easier to enforce the law against a youngster whose father is an alcoholic with a criminal record, than to enforce the same law against a youngster whose father is a lodge brother of the judge and makes large contributions to the political machine which controls the town. This is just one illustration of the fact that justice, far from being blind, is frequently cross-eyed, looking past the crimes of the "powerful" while gluing her eyes on those without power.

The second commandment describes the obligations of the Christian to speak up against all wrong—whoever does it. This is revolutionary; this is what makes Christianity, if it is reintroduced into Christendom, more powerful than the atomic bomb.

Here God works through us, and with us, if we are willing to become his tools and instruments. This ne has done many times in the past, often using the Christian conscience to start great social revolutions. Great Christian personalities have contributed to the abolition of slavery and the establishment of equal rights for women. It is significant that the only courageous white spokesman whom the Hereros of Southwest Africa have found is an Anglican clergyman, the Rev. Michael Scott. They are a people who have been robbed of their land and their rights as human beings by the Union of South Africa, in defiance of the United Nations. But the United Nations has not sent an army to defend the

Herero people, because the Union of South Africa is anti-Communist, and it is stylish to be anti-Communist today. Our free press has buried the story among the cooking recipes and the society news. It is easy to be against communism in America today; it is, in fact, the cheapest way to become popular.

But the second commandment calls us to speak up against unrighteousness wherever we find it, to speak for the downtrodden, the exploited, the hungry and the naked everywhere. If we are not willing to let God work through us, Luther says, "God will, after all, perform the work alone, and help the poor, and those who were unwilling to help him and have despised the great honor of doing his work, he will condemn with the unrighteous, because they have made common cause with the unrighteous." [5] This was the experience of the Israelites; God punished them through people who were worse than they were, namely through the Babylonians and Assyrians. This was the experience of the Romans, and of the French, and of the Germans— and it may become our experience as well. God's will will be done whether we are willing to be his instruments or not. If we are not willing, we are like the fig tree that does not bring forth fruit and is hewn down and cast into the fire.

Our responsibility to speak for the truth extends also into the realm of the church. Whenever the church becomes a social club, or a lecture hall on popular psychology, we have a responsibility to speak up for

[5] A Treatise on Good Works, p. 219.

truth in the church. It is the church in particular which is to praise and glorify God's name, and yet the church is often busy doing everything else but that. It is here that we as Christians have a responsibility *to keep the church the church.* The criterion, the standard, is always the Gospel of our Lord Jesus Christ.

Here it is important to note that the way to social justice goes through obedience to Christ, and not past or around him. The tragedy of the men and women who thought that they could save the world through the social gospel forty years ago was that they believed that the social gospel meant less emphasis on Gospel and more emphasis on sociology. As a result a great number of poor theologians with an incoherent and watered-down faith were created; consequently the zeal for improving society was also soon watered down.

If we are ever to make a Christian impact upon the community, we shall have to be more serious in our faith in our divine Lord. Only through him and from him can we receive the strength to influence the social order. Only a church that is faithful to her divine Saviour will be a church that is competent to promote justice and righteousness. If we want to improve the world through our *humanism,* because we believe men are by nature good and made evil only by forces over which they have no control, we shall soon "run out of gas" and our disappointment in men will turn us into cynics. If we want to change the world because of our Lord's command and in his power, we shall soon discover that he truly has the power to change things.

There is no more radical person than Jesus Christ. Compared with him all the world's radicals are mere conservatives. But his power is effective in us only as long as we believe him with all our being.

It is because our Lord Jesus Christ is the Son of God and our Saviour that we know that his way is the true way. Only in his power do "The blind receive their sight, and the lame walk, the lepers are cleansed, and the deaf hear, the dead are raised up, and the poor have the gospel preached to them." [6] Only through Christ can we see the signs of the kingdom until finally we shall see "a new heaven and a new earth . . . the holy city, new Jerusalem, coming down from God out of heaven, prepared as a bride adorned for her husband. And I heard a great voice out of heaven saying, Behold, the tabernacle of God is with men, and he will dwell with them, and they shall be his people, and God himself shall be with them, and be their God." [7]

The second commandment describes our relationship to God: we must praise and glorify him and pray to him in all trouble and need. It also shows our relationship to the world. Christians may not live their lives in isolation but are responsible for the world. Faith must always be active in love. "Let your light so shine before men, that they may see your good works, and glorify your Father which is in heaven." [8]

[6] Matthew 11:5.
[7] Revelation 21:1-3.
[8] Matthew 5:16.

CHRISTIAN WORSHIP

The Third Commandment: "Remember the Sabbath day, to keep it holy."

For Luther the third commandment is the commandment which describes our attitude toward God in works. In the first commandment, he says, "is prescribed our hearts' attitude toward God in thoughts, in the second, that of our mouth in words, in this third is prescribed our attitude toward God in works."[1] We must remember that we are talking about the Christian life, a life lived in faith. What does the third commandment then mean?

The life of faith is a life of worship. Worship is not a "law" forced upon people who are not willing to worship. Within the Christian life, within the life under the Gospel, worship is an expression of our faith and our love. We do not become Christians by worshiping; rather, because we are Christians we want to worship God. This is particularly true of prayer. Prayer is "a special exercise of faith," for where there is no faith,

[1] A Treatise on Good Works, p. 222.

there is no prayer. We may go through the motions out of habit, but we are not praying. Prayer is based on faith. On the other hand, that our faith may be weak and shaky is no reason for not praying. Even the smallest spark of faith is enough reason to pray and especially to pray for an increase in faith. Faith is trust in God which will grow as we pray for it. Luther points out that we do not pray because of our holiness, but we pray for holiness, because we are in need of it.

Jesus described our relationship to God in prayer as that of children speaking to their father whom they trust and love. This father deigns to hear anything that is on their hearts, even if it is foolish or dangerous. Thus God hears all our prayers. But this does not mean for a moment that he always does what we ask him to do, any more than a good father would fulfill all the wishes of his children even if he could do so. My six-year old might ask me for a revolver that shoots real bullets so that she can show the boys that she is a better cowboy than anybody else. I am glad that she asks me, that she has the confidence and trust in me which this request expresses, but for her own sake I will never grant this request.

God is not a celestial Sears Roebuck, to whom we send our orders and expect them to be filled by return mail. Such prayer is not the expression of trust and faith, but the expression of unbelief. If you give God orders instead of asking him and pouring out your heart to him, then you do not really believe that he is

Lord, that he knows what he is doing, but you think that you know better.

We can and must bring everything to God in prayer, for there is nothing so little and nothing so big that he will not hear us. But finally we must always say with our Lord Jesus Christ, who taught us how to pray, "Lord, not my will, but thine be done." This must be true of all of our worship and all of our prayer. Only through faith does the third commandment with all of its implications become a description of the Christian life. Thus Luther could say that the first, second and third commandments form one ring and chain of faith, describing the life which is lived in faith and where every action becomes a parable expressing the truth that God is love and has made his love known to us in Jesus Christ his Son. This is always the root and source of the Christian life.

What about the other commandments?

Looked at as expressions of the life under the Gospel, each of them describes what the love of God means in reference to other men when grasped in faith. When Christ is our Lord and in command of our life, all the relationships of our life necessarily change. As Christians we see all the natural relationships of life in a different light. Since Christ is Lord, in my family I must attempt to express the implications of this lordship. I must ask, what does it mean to me as a son or father, husband or wife, employer or employee, citizen or officeholder, pastor or church member, that Christ is Lord? This question is never merely theoretical, never a thought experiment. From the perspective of faith the commandments always become descriptions of what must and does happen in fact. The Christian faith is not a theory about life which is theoretically true or false. The Christian faith is life, and only true as it is lived. For the Christian life under the Gospel, the commandments are changed from "the law" into a description of the "good works" which must of necessity flow from faith in Jesus Christ.

THE CHRISTIAN UNDERSTANDING
OF AUTHORITY

The Fourth Commandment: "Honor thy father and thy mother that thy days may be long upon the land which the Lord thy God giveth thee."

If we now look at the other commandments in faith we find in each a clue to this new life. The fourth commandment speaks of the fact of authority. The authority of parents over children becomes symbolic for all other authority, the authority of our teachers, of our superiors, of all political authority. Of course all men, with the exception of a few anarchists, recognize some authority. As Christians we are asked to do more than merely submit to authority wherever that is unavoidable: we must see an opportunity for Christian service in all positions of authority as well as all positions where we are subordinated to authority.

Nothing seems to be harder for us Americans than to come to a positive evaluation of authority. The very word reminds us of dictatorship and concentration camps. However, as Christians we ought to know that the authority of law is the only possible protection against the usurpation of authority by a dictator or demagogue. The Christian does not reject authority but rather attempts to see all authority in reference to the Christ who is the source of all authority. The Word of God asserts that all legitimate authority has its source in God and is justified in dependence upon him.

Therefore, for the Christian the family is not merely a "biosocial" or "sociocultural" group but also the means through which children are brought into the fellowship of the church, where they should experience the combination of love and authority which will make it possible for them to pray "Our Father, who art in heaven" and not merely mumble meaningless phrases. And since for the Christian parental authority participates in God's authority, it is hard to defend an organization of the family which is complete anarchy.

It seems significant that today the enemies of the Christian church are more aware of their need to destroy the authority of the family than Christians are of their responsibility to maintain it. Wherever totalitarianism and secularism attack, they attack the family first. They realize that the Christian family, where parents and children love each other, is the most dangerous cell of opposition to a government that attempts to subordinate everything and everybody to the total state. Wherever parents and children trust and love each other the state cannot penetrate with its thought control and secret police. This kind of family relationship must be destroyed. Children are taken away from their parents to be educated and controlled entirely by the school and the youth organizations of the totalitarian government. Fathers and mothers are encouraged to live their lives apart from their children and also apart from each other so that the family as a living unit is destroyed. This was the pattern in Nazi Germany and still is in Soviet Russia. Children are to spy on their parents and report them to the secret police. Everything is done to destroy the influence and unity of the family, because it is man in isolation, when he does not think of himself as a member of a family, who is most susceptible to the blandishments of a state that wants to be mother and father and the source of all authority.

There are forces in America working, intentionally or inadvertently, toward the destruction of the family and thus sowing the seeds of destruction for our religious and political freedom. The finest school and the best-organized playground do not take the place of the family. As our American family disintegrates, the chances for the survival of our way of life diminish steadily. When the home becomes merely a dormitory where the members of the family sleep together, the time is ripe for the complete destruction of the strongest natural unit that opposes the complete control of man by the state or the party.

Christians will have to proclaim in an age which despises all authority that the authority of the family is from God. More effective than any such proclamation is the example of the Christian family, where the parents love and respect each other and where the children obey their parents in love and not in slavish fear. Here is a living sign to all the enemies of the Christian home that "to honor father and mother" is not a quaint archaic behavior pattern but the eternal will of God for his people. In this commandment as in all others, it is true that if it is seen from the perspective of faith it does not merely proclaim propositions about the true nature of the family but if enacted by the Christian it *is* the Christian family and a living witness to the power and grace of God. The Christian life is a life of discipleship within the natural framework of the family.

Similarly, the fourth commandment describes the Christian's attitude toward the reality of political authority. Also in the realm of political power as one who rules and as one who is ruled, the Christian expresses his faith in Jesus Christ by his life in this realm. For him the political realm is not some horrible snakepit from which he hopes to be redeemed but a realm in which the fact that Christ is Lord and Saviour is relevant and must be lived. Far from destroying the authority of government, the Christian citizen attempts to show with his life that the power of government is also borrowed power and is, as Paul never fails to emphasize, ultimately dependent upon and derived from the power of God.

It is fatal and futile if Christian people attempt to withdraw from the reality of political authority. Some have tried it by simple geographical removal from the governments they disapproved of. Mennonites, Quakers, and others have thought that an escape from the problems of political power is possible, but in the long run their attempts have been utterly futile.

In the United States today every American is involved in his government by paying its bills even if he never votes and never attends a political caucus. The only choice that we actually have is involvement, responsible or irresponsible. This is equally true of those who attempt to escape the ambiguities of the political life by ignoring it. Those Christians who say, "Politics is evil, we must not get involved in it," are expressing opinions on a controversial subject but are in no position to implement these with action. As we have said again and again, you do not escape a problem by ignoring it. Your very failure to participate is an attempt at solving the problem. For example, the Christian citizens of Chicago cannot excuse themselves from the political corruption in their city by saying, "We never vote." Such an excuse only betrays how guilty they are of the situation they try to ignore. The Christian life must be lived in the world. Every Christian has a responsibility to leaven the society in which he lives, including the political area.

Again Christian obedience is not merely the acceptance of some theoretical propositions about the nature of the state and of government. It is not enough to accept or reject some theories about the divine right of kings or for that matter the divine right of majorities. Again we must stress that the Christian life is never so theoretical. Since it is always discipleship, it is also discipleship in the field of politics; and the fourth commandment describes the responsibility of Christian men and women to be disciples as voters and candidates—in our particular form of government—just as they are to live their discipleship as parents and children.

Our church has been plagued by people who have had very comprehensive theories about the relationship of church and state but who never actually related their Christian faith to the community in which they wrote their impressive volumes on church-state relations. There is no such thing as theoretical Christianity; it is as real as the events upon which it rests. There cannot be a theoretical incarnation or a theoretical resurrection. Only as events, never as theories, are these words meaningful to Christians. Similarly the Christian life is meaningful only as it is lived in fellowship with God through Jesus Christ. It may be possible to be theoretically a Buddhist or a Confucian, a Thomist or a Barthian—but it is never possible to be theoretically a Christian. As the Christian faith stands on events that either occurred or did not occur and cannot be watered down to some theories about the nature of God, man, and the universe, so the Christian life is discipleship in all the walks of life and not some theory about the nature of the family or the state which may be theoretically accepted, but not lived in everyday life.

THE CHRISTIAN UNDERSTANDING OF COMMUNITY

The Fifth Commandment: "Thou shalt not kill."

We find the same truth applicable to all the other commandments. The fifth commandment, looked at as law, is merely the prohibition against taking human life. As such it belongs with the natural law which we discussed and which we believe to be written into the hearts of all men. But for the life under the Gospel the fifth commandment is no longer "natural law," but the description of the way in which our Christian faith can and must be lived in the local, the national and the international community. If we are the disciples of our Lord Jesus Christ it is not enough "not to do our neighbor any bodily harm or injury." We will show that the love of Christ is in our hearts by "assisting and comforting him in danger and want."

This means that the Christian life can never be lived in isolation from other men. There is no such thing as a Christian life which is merely a relationship between the individual and God. "If any one says, 'I love

God,' and hates his brother, he is a liar; for he who does not love his brother whom he has seen cannot love God whom he has not seen." [1]

All this has very practical consequences for our day-to-day life. Here we reject all efforts to reduce the Christian faith to the assurance of what has been derisively called "pie in the sky by and by." Enemies and friends of the Christian church have at times urged such an interpretation. Some have felt that it would protect the interests of the Christian church if she would not get involved in the ugly controversies which fray the tempers of people on weekdays. The church should deal only with people in Sunday clothes and with Sunday problems on their minds, and thus retain the respect and admiration of all people.

Enemies of the church have advocated the same as they pursued their dreams of power because they did not want to be bothered by the troubled Christian conscience. This was very interestingly demonstrated in the church struggle in Germany during the Nazi regime. Here some very fundamentalist sects met with the greatest approval of the Nazi leadership because they were satisfied to live their Christian life hidden in some corner far removed from the everyday problems of the German people. Nothing they said interfered in the slightest with the schemes of the Nazi Party and the relevance of the fifth commandment to the daily decisions of the German people was nicely camouflaged. The church struggle in Germany started

[1] I John 4:20.

when Christian people began to realize that the fifth commandment is relevant in the treatment of Jews by Germans. It is not enough to refrain from killing or not to do any bodily harm, but to help and comfort the neighbor in danger and want is of the very essence of the Christian life.

What was so spectacularly shown in Germany under the Nazis is equally true in America. As Christians we have a responsibility to see that laws are enforced and that our communities are justly administered. It is not enough to be concerned with the law enforcements in the suburbs where so many of us live; we are responsible for law enforcement on the other side of the tracks as well. In addition to law enforcement, the fifth commandment involves responsibility for the amelioration of every human need. Flood control, the fight against polio, slum clearance and traffic control all are Christian responsibility if the fifth commandment is seen as the description of the life of faith.

But more than that, it is not sufficient to be nominally concerned with all these worthy causes. One of the great dangers of this age of super-organization is that we have delegated the Christian fulfillment of the fifth commandment to agencies that are to fulfill it for us. Often we show no love in our personal relationships but we contribute to worthy causes who love for us. Though it is doubtless our duty to contribute generously to all these necessary agencies for the relief of human want and suffering, we would be gravely mistaken should we believe that such contributions free us from our personal responsibilities to show love to the neighbor. Agencies and organizations must supplement our personal works of love but they can never take their place. The fact that certain jobs are too big for us to do alone does not release us from our responsibility to do the many things that we can do as individuals. Contributions to foreign missions do not absolve us from our own personal responsibility to be missionaries wherever we go. Even the most generous support of agencies that combat racial discrimination does not relieve us from our own responsibility to show Christ's love to all men in our daily life.

Finally, the test of the fifth commandment as fulfilled in Christ and in the Christian comes in our relationship to all those people who to us are clearly unlovable. Luther says that tolerance of those who do us no harm is indeed quite easy: "Such meekness irrational animals have, lions and snakes, . . . knaves, murderers, bad women. These are all content and gentle when men do what they want or let them alone; and yet there are not a few who, deceived by such worthless meekness, cover over their anger and excuse it saying: 'I would indeed not be angry if I were left alone.'" And Luther continues: "Certainly, my good man, so the evil spirit also would be meek if he had his own way." [2]

The crux of the Christian fulfillment of the fifth commandment is its application to those who are our enemies. Our enemies are the very touchstone of the

[2] A Treatise on Good Works, p. 272.

Christian life. Out of our own power we can indeed love the good, the beautiful, the lovable, but it is only through the power of faith in Christ that we can love those who hate us and who are, humanly speaking, utterly unlovable. Such love was to the Greeks degrading. They measured the value of love by the value of the object loved. Only the love to the perfect was perfect and therefore only the love to God was ultimately justified.

But for us who have been made disciples of the Christ who is love, the goodness of the object of our love means little. Our love depends not upon the worth or beauty of the object but upon the reality and strength of the love of God working in us. In faith we become able so "to fear and love God as not to do our neighbor any bodily harm or injury, but rather assist and comfort him in danger and want." And the neighbor is every individual who needs our help, be he friend or foe, good or bad, in our home town or five thousand miles away.

THE CHRISTIAN AND SEX

The Sixth Commandment: "Thou shalt not commit adultery."

The Christian life under the Gospel recognizes the reality of sex. This statement might sound all too obvious to us but we should remember that at times certain people have considered sex in itself to be evil and sinful. Some Christians today consider the sexual instinct the source of all sin and the original sin a sexual sin. To them the only truly holy life is lived if one remains a celibate and attempts to ignore or fight the reality of sex during his life. Here sex and sin are substantially identified, and it is therefore impossible for such people to speak of a Christian life which would utilize the reality of sex in faith to the glory and praise of God.

In their obsession with sex as evil and the source of all evil these people are very similar to the Freudians, who also make sex the dominant factor in all life and explain all art and literature as well as all human action in terms of the sex drive. Both center life around sex, either negatively or positively. But whether you spend your days fighting your sexual instincts like some of the hermits of old or cultivating them like the hero of a modern psychoanalytic novel, sex instead of God becomes the center of your life. If one reads the writings of the modern Catholic authors such as Paul Claudel, one has the feeling that the Christian life exhausts itself in the struggle against sex, just as vainly as the efforts of a modern devotee of the libido who is forever seeking the complete fulfillment of his sexual desires. The Christian life of faith *includes* the reality of sex and subordinates it to the relationship of faith and trust in God which must dominate all life.

It is part of God's creative will that there should be man and woman. Not the devil but God created the fact of our dependence upon each other. There is nothing dirty or mean about this divine creation. The family which is sanctioned and protected in the fourth commandment derives its existence from the fact of sex.

According to God's creative will sex is channeled in the relationship of men and women into the institution of marriage. Marriage in some form as the ordered relationship of the sexes exists everywhere. There are no "noble savages" who live like animals, for man has everywhere circumscribed the relationship of the sexes with very definite rules. We Christians believe the monogamous marriage to be instituted by God.

As Luther puts it in the Large Catechism: "Therefore [God] also wishes us to honor [marriage] and to maintain and use it as a truly divine and blessed estate; because in the first place he has instituted it above all others, and therefore created man and woman [as is evident] not for lewdness, but to live in the married relation, be faithful, beget children, and nourish and train them to the glory of God. . . . Therefore I have always taught that this estate be not despised nor held in disrepute, as is done by the blind world and our false spiritual guides; but that it be regarded according to God's Word, by which it is adorned and sanctified, so that it is not only placed on an equality with other conditions in life but that it transcends them all, whether they be that of emperor, prince, bishop, or whatever they will."

However, marriage and fidelity in marriage are still part of the law; there is nothing specifically Christian about them. It is the sign of the Christian life to live in marital fidelity and love in such a manner as to give ever-new meaning to the many figures of speech which we find in the New Testament comparing the relationship between Christ and his church to perfect married life. Sex must become a valid aspect of this divinely ordained relationship. It is part of the story, but not the whole story. It is therefore false to make the propagation of the species the sole purpose of sex and marriage. And it is unexcusable when the mere fact of childlessness is made a basis for the annulment of a marriage. It is interesting to note that those Christians who deprecate sex and those who make it the center of all life agree in their disdain for the marital relationship apart from its function for the propagation of the race. Neither has any use for this love-relationship apart from reward in either "passion" or children. But for the Christian life the genuine acceptance of sex in marriage as part of the divine will is all-important.

Man was not created to spend his life fighting his sexual instincts. Neither was he created to spend his life absorbed in his sexual urges. From the point of view of the Gospel, sex and marriage are a part of God's order of life through which men and women can serve God. But the purpose of man's life is to live in fellowship with God. It is the glorious opportunity of the Christian life to show how through faith the marital relationship can become a symbol of love, trust, and fidelity. Then a love song such as the Song of Solomon can become to Christians at the same time a song of praise to God's order of marriage and a sign and symbol of the relationship between Christ and his bride, the church. "Husbands, love your wives, as Christ loved the church and gave himself up for her, that he might sanctify her, having cleansed her by the washing of water with the word, that the church might be presented before him in splendor, without spot or wrinkle or any such thing, that she might be holy and without blemish. Even so husbands should love their wives as their own bodies." [1]

[1] Ephesians 5:25-28.

WORK AND PROPERTY

The Seventh Commandment: "Thou shalt not steal."

Wherever human beings live in society, property relationships create problems and are ordered by law. There is a difference between what is mine and what is yours and what is ours. These property relationships are not ordered in the same way in all places. There are always some who cannot own property. Sometimes the group that controls all property is very small indeed. Sometimes human beings themselves are considered property.

The seventh commandment, understood as law, tells all men that they have no right to take away property that belongs to somebody either by outright theft or by fraudulent and unfair business dealings. It may even imply, as some have held, that slavery is always wrong because it is an offense against this commandment.

But from the point of view of the Gospel and looked at in faith, the seventh commandment shows how the Christian life must bring God's redeeming power into all the poisoned areas of man's economic life. In discussing this commandment in his *Sermon on Good Works,* Luther spends no time with theft and robbery but discusses at length "benevolence," "greed," and "liberality."

There can be no doubt that the Christian witness is of the greatest importance in the economic realm. For it is here that so many of the conflicts among men have their origin. The New Testament says, "The love of money is a root of all evil." And we face social theories today which make all men merely economic animals and the laws of economics the supreme laws of human existence. To the Communists private property is the metaphysical source of all evil; to the capitalists it is the metaphysical source of all good. Again, as in the realm of sex, Christians confront two contradictory interpretations both of which are dangerous and false, because they are making something which is an important *part* of life—property—the all-important *center* of life. Both groups are using alleged "economic laws" and making them the ultimate laws of the universe. To the Communists the laws of dialectic materialism, as set forth by Karl Marx and further interpreted by Lenin and Stalin, are the eternal will and law of the godless universe. All efforts to see life in broader terms than merely the narrow view of dialectical materialism are heresy, or as they like to say "deviationism." Art and literature, religion and morality are all forced into the narrow confines of this economic thinking.

Similarly a convinced laissez faire capitalist believes in the alleged law of supply and demand as the source of all goodness, truth, and justice. Like "private property" for the Communist, interference with this "law" is the original sin from which all other evils derive. Here, too, man is seen primarily as an economic being and the importance of economic laws is exaggerated until they become the absolute center of human existence.

Against all this pan-economic thinking the Christian fulfills the seventh commandment by showing in his life that God and not some alleged economic laws must be the focal point of human existence. The law of supply and demand must be subordinated to man's responsibility under God to love the neighbor. No economic theory must ever make human beings for whom Jesus Christ died into mere commodities to be used as means to economic ends. It makes little difference whether the end for which human beings are used is the dictatorship of the proletariat or the acquisition of wealth in the hand of capitalists, for the Gospel says "no" to all attempts to subordinate man's eternal purpose to love and glorify God to any particular economic theory.

In this conflict it is the task of the Christian to show through his daily life that God is the true center of all human existence. Economic and political power or wealth are never ends in themselves but are for the Christian means and talents which he must use to glorify his God and Saviour. And the Christian also knows that no property is ever truly "private." Since everything we own is held in trust from God we have no right to use it or waste it as if it were absolutely our own. This will have implications for soil conservation and many other specific problems. The Christian will always know himself a steward of God's gifts. He will always be aware of the fact that he must some day give account of his stewardship. Neither the abolition nor the glorification of private property, but life in fellowship with God is the way out of man's predicament. Man's problem is not essentially economic but theological, and no economic panacea touches the root of his anxiety and frustration.

In the light of the Gospel the economic life is understood from the point of view of the Christian concept of "calling" or vocation. It cannot be denied that men must work in order to live. Work is more than a necessary evil; it gives meaning and purpose to lives which would otherwise be utterly futile. But work is neither merely a means to acquire property nor a means to serve the state or the party; rather it is an opportunity to serve God. The Christian concept of "calling" means that through faith every Christian can and must see his daily work as an opportunity to serve God.

The particular character of the work makes little difference indeed. Through faith it is possible to see not only the more spectacular professions of the surgeon, the statesman, the pastor, and the missionary as avenues of Christian service, but also the truck driver, the riveter, the clerk, and the janitor. A job is a calling not by virtue of its own inherent character but by virtue of the Christian understanding of the jobholder. Every work done to the glory of God and in the service of our fellow-man is a Christian calling. And no job done for merely selfish purposes is holy by its nature. The work of pastor or missionary, of nurse or doctor is not inherently more of a Christian calling than any other human endeavor. If done in an egocentric manner without faith, the very proclamation of the Gospel fails to be a Christian calling. Indeed a man could baptize more people than the Apostle Paul, but if he does it without faith his work would be no more Christian than the faithless performance of any other skill or trade. It is not the work but the faith of the worker which gives an occupation its distinctly Christian character. The fulfillment of the seventh commandment in faith means that all our life becomes a living witness to the fact that Christ is our Lord and we are his disciples.

In factory and farm, in office and kitchen, Christians will show forth in their daily work that all work must be done for God's sake. There is no realm of labor where God is not Lord. It is impossible to say as a Christian, "Business is business" or "Politics is politics," as if there were areas of life which can operate according to their own rules and independent from the will of God. And, because the Christian faith is never a theory about life but a life of discipleship, it is not enough to acknowledge the lordship of Christ in all areas of life as a theoretical proposition which we consider true. The Christian life must be a life in which this lordship of Christ is acted out. There must be a difference in the way in which he who is a Christian does his job. This does not mean that he is expected to interrupt his activities as a welder every half hour to address a sermonette to his fellow workers. It means, however, that he will be the best welder he knows how to be because he is welding to the glory of God and sees in his daily work an opportunity to glorify God and serve his neighbor.

The seventh commandment is fulfilled whenever we do our daily work, not for the sake of the boss or for public acclaim or in order to become rich, but because we have understood that our daily work gives us an opportunity to give thanks with our work for all God has done for us.

"Thou shalt not steal." Fulfilled through the Gospel this means to work hard and well, not in fear of men but to the glory of God and in love to our neighbor.

INTEGRITY

The Eighth Commandment: "Thou shalt not bear false witness against thy neighbor."

All human society is based upon at least a minimum of honesty. Were men not generally honest in the use of their symbols (words) they could not even talk to each other. Language itself in order to be meaningful implies a minimum of honesty. Even a liar can only operate successfully because people generally mean what they say.

All social organization is based upon a certain amount of trust, so that society is in danger when this basic minimum of human honesty evaporates. It is for this reason that every society makes perjury a crime and insists on "bearing true witness" at least when the essential interests of society are at stake. There is nothing specifically Christian about not bearing false witness. It is part of God's law for all men in order to make ordered human life on earth possible.

What does the eighth commandment mean once it is looked upon from the point of view of faith? What does it say about the Christian life under the Gospel? It describes the Christian life as a life where language, understood in its widest sense, is used to the glory of God and in the service of the neighbor, that is, in truth. Luther in his *Treatise on Good Works* relates this commandment very clearly to the Christian responsibility for truth. He says, "Where such faith and confidence (in Christ) are, there is also a bold, defiant, fearless heart, that ventures and stands by the truth, though it cost life or cloak, though it be against pope or kings; such was the action of the martyrs. For such a heart is satisfied and rests easy because it has a gracious, loving God. Therefore it despises all the favor, grace, goods and honor of men, lets them come and go as they please; as is written in Psalm 15: 'He contemneth them that contemn God, and honoreth them that fear the Lord.' That is, the tyrants, the mighty, who persecute the truth and despise God, he does not fear, he does not regard them, he despiseth them; on the other hand those who are persecuted for the truth's sake, and fear God more than men, to these he clings, these he defends, these he honors, let it vex whom it may."

This commandment has all kinds of implications for the Christian's responsibility in art and literature, in science and history, and for freedom in general. Frequently in history Christian people have felt that such matters were none of their business or that they had an obligation to suppress truth for the sake of some ecclesiastical line of propaganda. Whenever this has happened the eighth commandment has been trans-

THE LIFE OF MAN UNDER THE GOSPEL

gressed. The Christian life under the Gospel must concern itself with the use of language for the sake of truth. The realm of literature has always been a place where Christians have tried to serve the truth. From the writings of the early church fathers to those of Dorothy Sayers and C. S. Lewis today, Christian people have attempted to bear witness to the truth in prose and poetry. Similarly and perhaps more indirectly through pictorial art, architecture and music, through scholarly research in the humanities and the sciences, Christians have fulfilled the eighth commandment in faith.

The commandment subjects Christians to close scrutiny. Can we still consider ourselves to serve truth if we write dishonest books—even though they have a pretty Christian lesson at the end? Do we serve Christ if we build dishonest buildings and perhaps especially dishonest churches, even though they are popular with people that know nothing about architecture? Can we consider ourselves serving Christ if we depict him the way the people who publish religious art think Christ should look for the greatest sales-appeal? Must an artist not paint Christ as he knows him to be out of the depth of his artistic and Christian inspiration?

Fulfilling the eighth commandment involves a witness to the truth not only "against popes and kings"— who are not very frightening to us in America at the present—but also against public opinion polls and congressional investigation committees. This brings us to the entire question of "freedom." To live the eighth commandment means also to defend men's integrity and right to search for truth even though their search may lead them far away from what we know to be the truth. Not to bear false witness means also that we must not attempt to tell people that truth can be found by accepting implicitly the opinions of people who have the truth. You cannot inherit truth; you cannot learn truth as you can learn the Gettysburg Address. Ultimate truth must be believed. Nobody can be forced to believe, and any effort to bring about faith in this manner is a tragic offense against the eighth commandment. If God refused to force men into faith, who are we to dare to tamper with a human integrity which God himself respected? The Christian faith has always made its greatest impact when it was seen as a clear alternative to other faiths. In the chaos of faiths in the Mediterranean world of the first three centuries, Christianity emerged victorious. When accepted merely as part of our heritage the Christian faith decays.

Again, the Christian life fulfills the eighth commandment when Christians live as courageous witnesses to the truth. To witness for truth means not only to declare our theoretical concern for truth, but also to show in every action that we believe that the God who revealed himself in Jesus Christ is truth, and that we have infinite respect for this truth, and that we will live the truth in all areas of life. Not by accepting propositions about God as true do we serve him in truth, but by letting his truth work in us so that in every act of our lives we bear witness to the truth.

COVETOUSNESS

The Ninth and Tenth Commandments: "Thou shalt not covet."

Confronted by these commandments we would do well to admit that all human life is dominated by covetousness. Whether we call it "will to power" or "libido" or "desire for happiness," man's life is impelled by the passion to get what others have. The last two commandments describe this sin which is at the root of many other sins. For even in our relationship to God we are always in revolt because we covet his divinity. From Adam and Eve, who desired to be "as gods" (Genesis 3), to the modern thinkers who claim loudly that man is God, human beings have always resented that they are creatures dependent upon God in every way.

In relationship to our neighbor we are dominated from childhood on by the desire to have what the other person has. We are not truly interested in the objects themselves as much as in having that which belongs to somebody else. One does not have to be around children for a long time in order to notice that even a small child desires the toy which the other child has and also that the chief attraction lies in the very fact that the other child has this toy. It is covetousness rather than the inherent value of the object which creates the interest.

This attitude stays with us all our lives. When we become older our boy friends or girl friends are often selected by virtue of their popularity with other girls and boys. We want the girl who goes with our best friend, or the fellow who dates our roommate. The object of interest has changed, but its covetous character has not. Later in life we begin to buy things for which we have no use whatsoever only because we want to have what somebody else has. Under the fancy title of "conspicuous consumption" an entire civilization can be described as being based essentially upon a form of covetousness.

It is possible to develop this basic human covetousness into individual or social "virtue." When we speak in glowing terms of the profit motive as the basic motive of our society, we have in fact elevated individual covetousness into the chief social virtue. Similarly if we glorify the interests of our nation or of our social class, and make them the chief motivating forces in our life, we have elevated group covetousness into the basic "life force."

Such an attitude may be very realistic. It may even be unavoidable because of the basic attitude of sinful man. Any effort in the direction of successful social organization must probably come to terms with this essential human covetousness. It seems that the Christian church with its appeal that Christianity is metaphysical fire insurance has also frequently used this arch-covetousness for its own purposes.

But is there nothing else that can be said about this state of affairs on the basis of the Gospel?

It seems clear that even the church's use of covetousness to drive people into its fellowship is clearly out of harmony with the Christian life of faith. For those who know that "he who shall seek his life shall lose it, and he who shall lose his life for Christ's sake shall find it," the individualistic or socialistic or ecclesiastical profit-motive must seem self-defeating. Even if we try to use this very word of Christ and attempt to turn it into some prudential prescription for finding our life, we are losing our life. The Apostle Paul says, "If I give away all I have, and if I deliver my body to be burned, but have not love, I gain nothing." [1] Covetousness in whatever form it may appear—and even in its most ecclesiastical garb—always separates man from God.

But what is the fulfillment of these commandments when Christ is our Lord in faith? As the Apostle Paul indicates, and as the entire New Testament clearly proclaims, the basic motive of our life must change. If we believe in Christ—if we are his disciples and his power dwells in us—then love that serves the neighbor becomes the basic force in our life. Instead of an

[1] I Corinthians 13:3.

individualistic, socialistic, or even ecclesiastical profit-motive, the motive of our life must be the love that is in Christ Jesus and that seeks the interest of the neighbor. This is the meaning of "repentance," or the "new direction of mind," of which the New Testament speaks so often. Our life is now directed not toward our own interest but toward the interest of those around us. We become extroverts in the most profound sense of this word. We lose our life daily to serve those who need us. In this sense Jesus Christ was the greatest "extrovert" who ever lived, for he lived only for the sake of others.

If rightly understood, this Christian love in fulfillment of the eighth and ninth commandments will transform all our life and give it an entirely new direction. Instead of using everything and everybody for our own advantage, we will let God use us for the advantage of our fellow-men and the proclamation of his kingdom. Everything that we have will become a means to make this service effective. Our house, our relationship to our wife or husband, all our possessions, are then means to show forth the power of the love of God. Just so in the life of Christ every human relationship and every possession from a marriage feast to a few loaves of bread and some fishes became an avenue for the proclamation of the good news of God's great love.

Again, the last two commandments are fulfilled in life, not in the theoretical disapproval of covetousness. The Christian faith when lived is not a theory about God's love but *is* the love of God in action through men and women who have become disciples of Christ. We must say it again: Christian faith is not a series of opinions about the nature of God, man and the universe; it is life as disciples of our Lord Jesus Christ, the Son of God, the Saviour. The theories are an attempt to describe what happens when Christ calls men to be his disciples. They may all be very true but they are no substitute for discipleship. A textbook on physiology is no substitute for living. No description, be it ever so accurate, of the eating process takes the place of eating. God sent his Son, a person who was born and lived and died and was raised again from the dead, in order that we might follow him by living our faith every moment of our life. Christianity is discipleship. This discipleship is only possible when God in his grace gives us the faith to see Christ as the Lord of our life.

ETHICS OF DECISION

Whenever the challenge of the life under the Gospel comes to us, we are overwhelmed by its possibilities and depressed by our own inability to live up to them. If we go through the Ten Commandments in faith we are at the same time exhilarated by the opportunity they describe and dejected by our own inability to live up to this opportunity. For no man ever lives un-ambiguously his faith in Christ in love towards his neighbor. As Christians we know that we are always unprofitable servants who cannot ever shake off the pride and covetousness which pervert all our actions. We know that in very one of our actions we operate with motives which come not from our faith but from our unbelief and revolt against God.

Furthermore, Christians are aware that this is not merely a personal inability to do the right thing but part of the human predicament. Often we don't have the choice between an action which is clearly good and one which is clearly evil, but with the best of intentions we are constantly confronted with the necessity to choose between two alternatives both of which seem evil. Perhaps this spectacular example may help to make it clear. I have a friend, a young American officer, whose job it was to organize the French Underground in its fight against the Nazi conquerors. For this purpose he jumped by parachute into occupied France and established contact with French peasants and workers who were hiding in the woods and mountains. After he had organized them into something of a fighting unit they would engage the Nazi occupation troops. Everybody was risking his neck. In this fighting no prisoners were taken. There were only victors and corpses. During one of these engagements when the Nazis were on their heels, the group under the command of my friend lost one man through injury. He could not be carried along. He had to be left behind. The question was—should he be left dead or alive? If alive, he would probably endanger the lives of all his comrades by revealing their names and hiding places under Gestapo torture. Yet this man was their friend—could they kill him in cold blood? What was right? My friend told me that they decided to hide him in the bushes on the side of the road, hoping that the Nazis would miss him. It worked. Would it have still been right if it had not worked and led to the execution of hundreds of men and their families?

Not all our decisions are similarly complex, but there is not one in which our selfishness and conceit are not involved in whatever we do, though it may look ever so "Christian" to the observer from the outside. Even the love of a mother for her child is often selfish in its exclusion of other children. Even the sacrifice of life for others is frequently tainted by the desire to receive publicity and praise either here or hereafter. In view of all this we are tempted to ask, "What's the use?" The Christian life would be worthwhile—but we are too weak, too selfish, too proud. It is not for us!

This would have to be our answer, were it not for the fact that the Christian life is lived not out of our own resources but out of the power and grace of God. It is through this power that it becomes possible for us to live the Christian life from day to day in spite of failures and sins that will always hamper and defeat us. The beginning, center, and end of the Christian life on earth is God's forgiveness in Jesus Christ as it has been revealed to us on the cross. Because of the cross and the power of him who died for us on the cross we can each day become Christians anew. This kind of Christian life is not some static possession which we have attained for all time and now merely passively enjoy. On the contrary, it requires a constant wrestling with the powers of evil that attempt to keep us in subjection. We never *are* Christians in the sense that we have arrived and can now rest on our laurels. We are always *becoming* Christians.

This dynamic view of the Christian life has been colorfully expressed by Luther in his explanation to the sacrament of baptism, when he says, "It signifies that the old Adam in us is to be drowned and destroyed by daily sorrow and repentance, together with all sins and evil lusts; and that again the new man should daily come forth and rise, that shall live in the presence of God in righteousness and purity forever." The Christian life is not retreat from the world; it is not the calm refuge of the desert island. It is conflict and tension, as Paul says, "For we are not contending against flesh and blood, but against the principalities, against the powers, against the world rulers of this present darkness, against the spiritual hosts of wickedness in the heavenly places."[1]

In this struggle we prevail because of the power of Christ and are not defeated because of the resource of his daily forgiveness which we receive in a unique manner through the sacrament of Holy Communion. It is because of this resource that in spite of our own weakness and incompetence we are not afraid to take on the enemy, trusting not in our own powers but in the power of God in Christ.

We are not defeatists when confronted by the challenge of the Christian life in a world that crucified Christ. The Christian realization of the ambiguity of the human situation and man's inability to extricate himself from it is not pessimism. It is the kind of realism that makes a successful battle possible. Not he who is overconfident, but he who knows his own weakness and resources is more likely to be victorious.

We have seen in our time the spectacular collapse of world-views placing trust in man and his powers. Nazism and Fascism were not victorious although they had the most optimistic view imaginable concerning

[1] Ephesians 6:12.

the possibilities of the German and Italian people. Even our own dreams of world peace and universal prosperity are severely shaken because they are based upon an overoptimistic view of men's rationality and good intentions.

Only upon the firm foundation of a sound analysis of the human situation can a meaningful life be built. The Word of God gives us this sound analysis, showing us what man can do and what he cannot do. It shows man's utter dependence upon the God who created him, preserves him, and wants to save him.

The Christian life is existence in the presence of this God. It is fulfillment of the law through the power of Christ "Who has redeemed us, lost and condemned creatures, secured and delivered us from all sins, from death and from the power of the devil, not with silver or gold, but with his holy and precious blood, and with his innocent sufferings and death, in order that we might be his, live under him in his kingdom, and serve him in everlasting righteousness, innocence, and blessedness, even as he is risen from the dead and lives and reigns to all eternity."

BIBLIOGRAPHY

Aristotle, *Nicomachean Ethics*. New York: Oxford Univ. Press. This is Aristotle's painstaking analysis of what constitutes "the good life."

Augustinus, Aurelius, *The City of God*. New York: E. P. Dutton, 1945. One of the great Christian theologians discusses, among other things, the Christian life.

Beauvoir, Simone de, *The Ethics of Ambiguity*. Citadel. The atheistic existentialist's explanation of the good life.

Bennett, John C., *Christian Ethics and Social Policy*. New York: Scribner's, 1946. An analysis of the various systems of social ethics developed during the history of the Christian church.

Bonhoeffer, Dietrich, *The Cost of Discipleship*. New York: Macmillan, 1951. A brilliant young German theologian, eventually murdered by the Nazis, calls for the imitation of Christ. "Cheap grace is the deadly enemy of our church."

Brunner, Emil, *The Divine Imperative*. Philadelphia: Westminster Press, 1947. An evangelical discussion of "What ought we do?" not only as individuals but as social groups.

Calvin, John, *Institutes of the Christian Religion*. Philadelphia: Westminster Press, 1936. The Swiss reformer's profound system of Christian theology, and in particular his description of the Christian life.

Forell, George W., *Faith Active in Love*. New York: The American Press, 1954. An examination of Luther's social-ethics by the author of this book which attempts to show that Luther's ethics was an ethics of decision.

Huxley, Julian S., *Man in the Modern World*. New York:

Mentor, 1948. Life from the point of view of biological naturalism, with a chapter on religion as an objective problem.

Kierkegaard, Søren, *Training in Christianity*. Princeton: Princeton University Press, 1944. Danish philosopher presents claim that the Christian life depends on Christ becoming our contemporary.

Kierkegaard, Søren, *Works of Love*. Princeton: Princeton University Press, 1946. Reflections on Christian love as the works of love.

Köberle, Adolf, *The Quest for Holiness*. Minneapolis: Augsburg, 1938. A biblical, historical, and systematic investigation of the relationship of justification to sanctification.

Lewis, C. S., *Christian Behaviour*. New York: Macmillan, 1943. Easily understandable and extremely lucid thinking on the Christian life.

Luther, Martin, *The Large Catechism*. Book of Concord, Vol. I. Philadelphia: Fortress Press. An explanation of the basic facts of the Christian faith which "of necessity every Christian should know; so that he who does not know this should not be reckoned among Christians, nor be admitted to the sacraments."

Niebuhr, H. Richard, *Christ and Culture*. New York: Harper, 1951. An examination of the various ways in which Christians have related faith and culture.

Niebuhr, Reinhold, *An Interpretation of Christian Ethics*. New York: Harper, 1935. The relationship between the absolute demands of the Gospel and all the relative situations in which these absolute demands confront us.

Nietzsche, Friedrich, "The Genealogy of Morals," in *The Philosophy of Friedrich Nietzsche*. New York: Doubleday. The most brilliant attack against the Christian life from the point of view of logical naturalism.

Nygren, Anders, *Agape and Eros*. Philadelphia: Westminster Press, 1953. An analysis of God's love as the source of all true love.

Patterson, Charles H., *Moral Standards*. New York: Ronald

BIBLIOGRAPHY

Press, 1949. An introduction to the problems of ethics for college students.

Plato, *The Republic, The Dialogues of Plato*. New York: Random House, 1937. The Greek philosopher's search for the nature of virtue and the perfect society.

Ramsey, Paul, *Basic Christian Ethics*. New York: Scribner's, 1950. Christian ethics as the ethics of "obedient love." An excellent text, marred by an entirely individualistic and subjectivistic concept of evil.

Russell, Bertrand, *Selected Papers*. New York: Modern Library, 1927. An honest atheist presents his case for continuing life.

Weil, Simone, *Gravity and Grace*. New York: G. P. Putnam, 1952. A sensitive young Jewish Frenchwoman wrestles with the meaning of life in a profoundly Christian way.

Wheelwright, Philip, *A Critical Introduction to Ethics*. New York: Odyssey Press, 1949. A survey of the problems of philosophical ethics.